The Clay Family

Part First - The Mother of Henry Clay
Part Second - The Genealogy of the Clays

Z. F. Smith
Mary Katherine Rogers Clay

Alpha Editions

This Edition Published in 2021

ISBN: 9789354410673

Design and Setting By
Alpha Editions
www.alphaedis.com
Email - info@alphaedis.com

PREFACE.

A FEW elderly citizens yet living knew Henry Clay, the renowned orator and statesman, and heard him make some of his greatest speeches. Younger persons who heard him not, nor saw him while living, have learned much of him through his numerous biographers and from the mouths of others who did know him. Most that has been known of him, however, by either the living or the dead, has concerned his political career. For the purpose of securing votes for him among the masses in his candidacy for different offices he has been represented by his biographers as being of lowly origin in the midst of impecunious surroundings. Such, however, was not the condition of his early life. He was of gentle birth, with parents on both sides possessing not only valuable landed estates and numerous slaves, but occupying high social positions. Indeed, he could look back upon a long line of ancestors from whom descended a family record worthy of being inherited.

The unapproachable eminence attained by Henry Clay as an orator and statesman has made every thing connected with him almost sacred. He has made us want to know something about every one bearing his name — every one in whose veins flows the Clay blood. We would know all that can be learned of his nearest of kin, and especially of that fortunate woman who brought him into the world. A mother who could give birth to such a son as Henry Clay deserves universal remembrance. But has this mother been awarded such remembrance? Who outside of some of her immediate descendants, perhaps, can tell the story of her life, recount her virtues, or even pronounce her maiden name? There are biographies enough of her illustrious son. A dozen or more of them are now before me, and some of them in more than one large volume; but some of them are silent even as to her name, while none of them devotes more than a sentence or paragraph to the mother of the hero they are striving for words to justly eulogize. One can scarcely learn from these biographies that Henry Clay had a mother at all, and they could certainly learn from none of them the womanly virtues which characterized this noble mother.

The Fourteenth Publication of the Filson Club, entitled "The Clay Family," supplies much of this lacking information. It is divided into two parts, and is by two different authors. Part First, by the Honorable

Zachary F. Smith, is devoted to the Clay and Hudson families generally, and especially to Elizabeth Hudson, the mother of Henry Clay. Part Second is by Mrs. Mary Rogers Clay, and embraces the genealogy of the Clays. Both parts were prepared for The Filson Club and are now published for the purpose of making them more accessible to the members than they could have been in a single manuscript filed among the archives of the Club.

Genealogy is now the fashion, and the Clay family affords a fine theme in this line. The Clays have had an enviable history in our country for more than two centuries, and although none other bearing the name has risen to the eminence attained by the "Sage of Ashland," a goodly number of them have filled positions of honor and trust which would shine more brightly but for the eclipsing rays of the "Great Commoner." All of the Clay family are interesting to us because of the good deeds of some of them and the bad deeds of none of them, and their genealogy can hardly fail to be acceptable to the members of The Filson Club.

The twenty illustrations of this publication will be found to be the best that can be produced in the half-tone style. It was much regretted that a likeness of the mother of Henry Clay could not be found to take its place in this work. Her illustrious son appears in a full-page halftone from an oil painting by the celebrated Matthew H. Jouett. Colonel Robert T. Ford, who has recently purchased of one of the Clays a large bluegrass farm in Bourbon County, Kentucky, kindly furnished for this publication a photograph of the original, which he owns, and it is believed that this is the first time this likeness of Henry Clay has been made public in book form.

It is not likely that The Filson Club will publish another book during the year of 1899. Taking into consideration the importance imparted to the subject by the world-wide name of Henry Clay, and the fame of other members of the family as cabinet officers and senators and representatives, and foreign ministers, and governors, and judges, and legislators, and soldiers, and men of affairs, it would seem that this fourteenth volume of The Filson Club publications may be esteemed one of the happiest of its series, and may be regarded as a fitting close of the good work of the Club in the century now rapidly approaching its end.

R. T. Durrett,

President.

Honorable ZACHARY F. SMITH.

PART FIRST

The Mother of Henry Clay

BY

Hon. Z. F. SMITH

Member of The Filson Club

The Mother of Henry Clay.

THE woman who gave to our republic its greatest statesman and orator — perhaps in all the most gifted of his generation — can not but be a person of interest to every Kentuckian, and indeed to every American citizen of to-day and of future time. Whether the masterly genius that moulded political sentiment, led great parties and policies through victory and defeat, and swayed the destinies of the nation for half a century was an ancestral heritage or the result of early parental training of mind and character, or both, the subject is interesting. It is worthy of more conspicuous mention upon the pages of history, as well as in the private realm of the literary circle.

The solitary greatness of Washington and the ingenerate exclusiveness of the family from which he sprang have led to inquiry that has given us some insight into the life and character of the woman who gave to our country the greatest of great men. But who can speak familiarly to-day of the mothers of Thomas Jefferson, of James Madison, or of others of the collegiate of statesmen who, under the inspiration of opportunity, proclaimed the gospel of personal and civil liberty but a little over a century ago? These have made illustrious the history of America. The irreverent neglect which has permitted the names of so many worthy women to pass from public view may too long and too fatally consign to oblivion the noble matron, the mother of the immortal Clay.

Virginia has been honorably mentioned as the "mother of States and the cradle of statesmen." Why not add: "And of immortal women"? In the year 1750, in the county of Hanover, in the grand old colony, was born Elizabeth Hudson, an event that, indirectly, was destined to play an important part in the history of the American people and of the nations of the world outside.

About the year 1700, John Hudson, a gentleman of English descent, settled in Hanover County, Virginia, and married Elizabeth Harris. There were born to these eight sons, Christopher, John, William, George, Charles, David, Cuthbert, and Thomas, besides three daughters, of whose names we have no record. One son, George Hudson, married Elizabeth Jennings and settled in the same county of Hanover, Virginia being then under the colonial government of England. The last named couple, George Hudson and Elizabeth Jennings, were the parents of Elizabeth Hudson and the maternal grandparents of

Henry Clay, afterward of Lexington, Kentucky, the orator and statesman. The Hudson family were possessed of a liberal estate of land and slaves, and lived in the somewhat pretentious style of the landed gentry of colonial days.

The accredited stories of the early life of Henry Clay having been cast in an environment of poverty and toil and sore want are apocryphal legends not sustained in the light of well-known family traditions and facts. His biographers have written more with a view to political effect than in the interests of the truth of historic research. It is more probable that the grandparents, at least, both paternal and maternal, were accustomed to drive in their coach-and-four with servants in livery, and to supply their costlier wardrobes and other elegancies and luxuries unobtainable at home from the shops of London and Paris. If this ostentatious style of living was later modified in the Clay family, it was because of the blighting presence of hostile armies during the War of the Revolution, carrying desolation to the homes of the people, as in the Southern States during the late Civil War. Hanover County was a part of the theater of campaign and strife in that struggle, as it was the border of strategic movement and bloody carnage in the later contest.

Elizabeth Hudson grew to womanhood and married Reverend John Clay, a minister of the Baptist Church. They first settled in Henrico County, Virginia. At this period religious proscription, though of a mild type, was rife in Old Virginia on the part of the established English Church against all dissenters. The Baptist preachers in those days had but a meager and feeble following. They even at times went to prison under the charge of disseminating pestilent heresies, as the orthodox orders were pleased to term their preaching. We readily infer that the Reverend John Clay was but poorly rewarded from the contributions of the brethren, and that he needed to look mainly to secular sources for the support of his household.

To the Reverend John and Elizabeth Hudson Clay were born nine children: Betsy Hudson, George Hudson, Henry, who died in infancy, John, Sally, Molley, Henry, Porter, and a posthumous child, a daughter. Betsy Hudson and the first Henry died before their father; George died just as he reached manhood, and the daughters died young and unmarried. Of the order of the ages of these we have no certain information, beyond the mention in the will of the father. We know that Henry Clay, our Great Commoner, was born April 12, 1777, and named after an older brother Henry, who died about four years or a little more before the death of his father. We also learn that Porter Clay was younger than Henry, and the youngest of the brothers.

The infancy of the Great Commoner began, therefore, in the midst of the scenes of the Revolution. Among the earliest impressions upon his mind were those made amid the turbulent strifes of insurrectionary war, never effaced in life. These cruel memories may have been largely the incentive to the passionate ardor and eloquence with which he urged war with England, on the floor of Congress, in 1812.

George Hudson and wife had another daughter, Mary, who married Captain John Watkins, of whom we shall have occasion to speak again. She was the elder sister of Mrs. John Clay. George Hudson was a staunch Tory in the Revolution, while his two daughters were pronounced rebels, and availed themselves of every opportunity to render aid and comfort to the struggling patriots. Divisions among neighbors and kindred and friends in the same communities and households were as common in that dramatic period as among their descendants in our later Civil War in the border Southern States.

Reverend John Clay, the father, died in 1781, when his son Henry had but reached his tender boyhood's fifth year of age, leaving Mrs. Clay a widow of thirty-one years. The strife and rage of war continued for one year after the sad event, until at last tidings of the surrender at Yorktown gave the inspiration of hope to the people that the angel of peace was nigh, with the promise of repose and security to the country. Authentic records and traditions give us the information that Reverend John Clay and family moved from their home in Henrico County to Hanover County in 1777, and settled at the old Hudson homestead farm, three and a half miles southeast of Hanover Court-House. Here Henry Clay was soon after born. The famous dwelling-house was destroyed by fire many years ago. This homestead Hudson plantation was to be disposed of by the terms of the will of George Hudson after the demise of his widow. But before such events Reverend John Clay purchased the undivided half interest of the other heirs, John Watkins and wife, and died before the same was paid for. A friendly suit was brought to legally settle the questions whether this plantation should be sold or disposed of under the provisions of the will of George Hudson or under the contract of sale to Reverend John Clay. The Court decided in favor of the latter, and, by its decree, the plantation was finally sold and purchased by Henry Watkins, who had then married the widow of John Clay.

Both George Hudson and his son-in-law, John Clay, were possessed of numbers of slaves sufficient to cultivate their plantations and to render such domestic service as was needed. Each disposed of thirty or more slaves in his will, most of them by names. From these facts, and from other sources, we readily infer that the home establishments were well supplied with the comforts of life, and that the members of these families were not strangers to such things of luxury as were attainable then, either at home or from the marts of Europe. There is a well-preserved family tradition that George Hudson lost eight thousand pounds sterling by security debts, a too common occurrence of loss in those days of neighborly accommodation.

The Clay posterity was well represented a century ago in our infant Commonwealth of Kentucky, in the families of General Green Clay, of Madison County; of Henry Clay, of Lexington; and of old Colonel Henry Clay, of Bourbon County, cousins not very remote and of nearly the same age. They were of goodly Welch ancestry, being descended from Sir John Clay, of Wales, whose sons came to America in the earliest years of the Seventeenth Century and settled on James River. In Volume I, page 18, of the Memoirs of Cassius M. Clay, we quote from a letter of Reverend Porter Clay, who was then preaching at Alton, Illinois, in 1848, as follows:

"In the reign of Queen Elizabeth, Sir Walter Raleigh brought over to the Virginia plantations, among others, three brothers, sons of Sir John Clay, of Wales, England. He gave them ten thousand pounds sterling each. They were named Charles, Thomas, and Henry. They settled on James River, near Jamestown. Charles and Thomas had large families. Henry had none, but the name has been handed down with great tenacity in both families ever since. Cassius M. Clay is a descendant of Charles Clay, Henry and myself from Thomas Clay."

In the same autobiographic memoirs, Cassius M. Clay has to say:

"I believe I have the only reliable record of the Clay family extant; and that our families (Henry Clay and General Green Clay) unite in my great-grandfather, Henry Clay, son of Charles, son of Sir John, of Wales. My grandfather was named Charles; his father, Henry; and his father again, Charles, who, with his two brothers Henry and Thomas, came to America. . . . My great-grandfather, Henry Clay, was born in 1672. The descending line after is all regular down to my birth in 1810."

The record given in the letter of Reverend Porter Clay is so brief as to be obscure on its first perusal. The Charles Clay from whom Cassius M. descended, and the Thomas (John, it should be) Clay from whom he and his brother Henry descended, as he mentions, are evidently not the sons of John who came over from Wales, but of Henry Clay, the great-grandfather of

Cassius M. and of Henry the Great. This construction partially agrees with the record written by General Green Clay, which we have. Both agree, or rather seem to agree, that the father of Porter and Henry Clay was Reverend John Clay; his father, John Clay; his father, Henry Clay, in whom the two lines meet. All agree that the first known ancestor was Sir John Clay, of Wales. In a recent letter E. F. Clay, of Paris, Kentucky, son of Brutus Clay and grandson of Green Clay, says of old Colonel Henry, of Bourbon County: "I have always heard that this branch of the Clay family was more closely related to the Great Henry than my own." The relation seems to be the same.

This "Old Henry," so called to distinguish him from the numerous Clay descendants of Bourbon County and elsewhere, was the son of Henry Clay, junior, M. D., and he the son of Henry Clay, senior, of Virginia, the great-grandfather of our Henry and of Cassius M. Clay. He was born September 14, 1779, in Virginia, and came to Kentucky in his eighth year of age with his father, Doctor Henry Clay, who settled southeast of Paris, in Bourbon County, in 1787. Doctor Henry, of Bourbon, was therefore a first cousin of General Green Clay and of Reverend John Clay, the father of our Henry. The Clay descendants are numbered by the hundreds in

Bourbon and adjacent counties, in the families of the Clays, the Bedfords, the Buckners, the Kennedys, the Lewises, the Woodfords, the Hedges, the Spears, the Rogers, and others beyond mention here.

On the authority of Reverend Porter Clay we are told that the first ancestors of all the Clay families of which we have made mention settled early in the Seventeenth Century in the Jamestown Colony, with a dole each of ten thousand pounds sterling, equal to fifty thousand dollars, from their father, Sir John, of Wales. If the Clays were as thrifty and provident at that end of the line as they are known to have been at this end for over a century, we may readily infer that the father of our Henry was established in Virginia with a comfortable estate of land and slaves when he was wedded to Elizabeth Hudson under English dominion. It is a remarkable fact that the splendid homestead farms acquired a century or more ago by the ancestors, respectively, of the three Kentucky families, among the best of our Bluegrass lands, are all to-day held and occupied by their descendants in direct line of succession. We mention these facts of ancestral history as conclusive evidence that the early boyhood life of Henry Clay was not cast in an environment of extreme poverty and enforced toil; nor were his lineal antecedents obscure and inconsequential. That he figures as "The Mill-Boy of the Slashes," riding to and from Mrs. Darricott's mill, on Pamonkey River, on a bag of grain, and assisted in the lighter work on the plantation, as represented by his biographers, we accept without question. Many now living know this to have been a common practice with boys reared upon farms by slave-owning parents.

What may have been the experiences of or the part taken by the Reverend John Clay in the Revolution, and the belligerent movements thereof, are questions about which our authorities are mainly silent. The noble dames of that period, however, with rare exceptions, were in alignment with their husbands on all party questions, and especially on the one that divided Tory and rebel. We have mentioned that Mrs. Clay was an irrepressible rebel; we may take for granted that her husband was not a Tory.

A thrilling episode of those days of peril, which the mother of Henry Clay often related in after life to her friends in Kentucky, shows that the family was not exempt from the sore trials incident to the pending strifes of war. Two accounts were given the writer, agreeing in the main, but each containing some details not related by the other. Both were given as heard from the lips of Mrs. Clay herself.

We have made mention of the untimely death of Reverend John Clay, leaving to the matronly young widow the care of their infant children and the burden of the management of the plantation and slaves. In the hours of bereavement and intensest grief the solemnities of the burial services were ended and the stricken household left alone to their first night of mourning. It happened that the British forces, known as Tarleton's troopers, were marauding in that section of Virginia at the time and committing many depredations. On the day after the burial a detachment of this command appeared upon the premises and began a series of outrages such as only a band of outlaws under military license could have been guilty of. Not satisfied with supplies of food for themselves and provender for their horses, they wantonly destroyed the widow's property, at the same time taunting her with brutal jibes and insults.

The story as first told to the writer was noted down nine years ago from the lips of Mrs. Lucy Trabue, of Bourbon County, formerly Miss Cosby, of Woodford County. Mrs. Trabue was at the time nearing her eightieth year of age. She was born and reared to young womanhood an intimate neighbor of the mother of Henry Clay, who was then Mrs. Henry Watkins. Mrs. Trabue's mind was a treasure-house of reminiscences of the olden times, and she could entertain a good listener by the hour with the relation of these.

When the detachment of loyalist troopers were seen approaching, there was but one white male person present, the overseer of the plantation. At the instance of Mrs. Clay he escaped by the back way and eluded capture. The soldiers, a number of whom were recruits from the country, unceremoniously entered the house and began their brutal work. They first ransacked the kitchen and larder, and satisfied their hunger. Next they turned their attention to the destruction of the furniture and to general pillage. Bureaus were chopped to pieces, trunks and chests broken open, and every room and closet ransacked for such articles of value as were portable. Other property which the vandals could not well carry off was wantonly wrecked and scattered about the house. One hundred years ago it was the custom of our grandames to provide a fat feather tick and a straw tick for each bed, and to alternate these for winter and summer. After breaking up the bed frames, the roystering troopers ripped open half a dozen of these feather ticks and emptied their contents out at the windows. The air was as thick with flying feathers as with leaves from the forest after an autumn frost. The remorseless raiders finally rode off with their stolen booty, to which they added scores of chickens and turkeys which they had killed. They carried off with them a number of the slaves of the plantation, how many we know not. These abducted slaves were most probably a small part of the many thousands forcibly borne away to Canada or England by the British armies during hostilities. In the execution of the treaty of peace, after the close of the war, the return of these to their owners was demanded on the plea that, under the laws of England and Virginia, they had always been recognized and held as property. The English Government, arrogant and insulting as it then was, refused to accede to this demand. In spirited retaliation the Virginia Assembly enacted a law preventing the collection of any debts due to English creditors by her citizens in the Virginia courts. In revenge for this law, the government of England refused to give up the forts on the lake borders on the territory ceded to the United States. This dead-lock was not broken for over ten years after the treaty was signed, and in all this time the British officials were arming and equipping stealthily the savage Indians to war on the whites along the border settlements, though they were sworn to observe the stipulations of peace. Kentucky bore the brunt of these Indian hostilities, and during the ten years four thousand of her citizens, men, women, and children, fell victims to savage barbarity through English malice and cruelty.

Mrs. Trabue remembered Mrs. Clay-Watkins as a very entertaining conversationalist. The flush of resentment would animate her features and flash from her eyes as she would recall the memories of these desecrations enacted at the sacred shrine of home and over the remains of her dead husband but barely cold beneath the sod. She remembered one incident not related by others, over which the heroic matron dwelt with more than usual pathos. Among the things of value of which her chests were rifled was her wedding dress, made of white satin and richly trimmed, and no doubt from the artist hands of some famous maker in London or Paris. It was a relic treasured with a tenderness of sentiment and pride which only a good woman can know who has been a bride, and beyond all earthly price to her alone. The ruffian who stole the endeared relic was an officer. He threw it across his saddle and mounted. The last wistful view of the beautiful robe was as he rode away, not to return. Mrs. Trabue said that as the venerable matron would come to this incident of her narrative her voice would tremble with tenderer emotion, while tears would fill her eyes and trickle down her cheeks.

We introduce now a letter of Mr. Thomas B. Watkins, a grandson yet living of Mrs. Clay-Watkins. It is dated "Lexington, Kentucky, September 19, 1894:"

"In reply to yours, I can only tell you a part of what my mother has many times told me. She was very intimate with my grandmother. The father of the latter was George Hudson, and her mother was Miss Jennings. There were two children born to them, Mary and Elizabeth. Mary married Captain John Watkins. You will find a trace of him in Collins' History, in mention of Woodford County.

"Elizabeth, the youngest, first married John Clay. Of the children born to them, I can give you the names of only four now, Henry, Porter, John, and Betsy. From the best information I have, she was rather below the medium in stature and of well rounded form, dark hair and eyes, and ruddy complexion. She was a woman of great determination, industrious and economical.

"She was born in 1750, and died in 1829. I have never heard of a picture or portrait of her of any kind. There may be some heirloom about Versailles. I can recall only one story told me by my mother. It occurred about the time of the death of her first husband, John Clay. Colonel Tarleton made a raid into Virginia and came to her place. Her husband had been buried the day before. Her children were all young and dependent. Aside from her own family, there was but one white person on the place, her overseer, whom she made leave by the back way.

"Tarleton's men searched her house. They ripped open her beds and emptied the feathers out of the windows, killed her fowls, and took away some of her slaves. One of the men threatened to, or did, thrust his sword into the new-made grave.

"She complained to Tarleton about this villainous treatment of a helpless woman. He told her to point out the guilty and he would have them punished. She reprimanded him roundly, and told him he knew it was impossible for her, during so much confusion, to point out the guilty ; they were all strangers to her and dressed alike. He then said : ' Madam, you shall be paid for your losses,' and at once had a sack of coin emptied on a table near by. She was afraid to openly refuse the money, but when Tarleton left, she scraped it off into her apron and cast it into the fire, saying her hand ' should not be polluted with British gold.'

"Her father was a Tory ; she and her sister ardent rebels. She had often taken a servant and pack-horse and traveled for miles from home, carrying provisions to the American soldiers.

"Her second husband was Henry Watkins, who was ten years younger than herself. A number of children were born to them. Four only lived to be of age : John, Frank, Nathaniel, and Patsey.

"George Hudson, her father, was of English descent. He had a liberal estate of lands and negroes, and lived in the best style of that day, drawing upon the mother country for such articles of luxury or fashion as were not obtainable at home."

The homestead plantation probably fronted on some river or considerable stream of water not always fordable. Our traditions repeat from Mrs. Clay-Watkins that she often ordered the servants to throw apples, potatoes, and other lighter food supplies across the river to the pickets and scouts of the patriot army when in that vicinity. On the other hand, when the enemy occupied and foraged the country, she had at times to bury from sight her bacon, provisions, and other things of value.

Of the brothers and sisters of Henry Clay, our information is meager. John is said to have most resembled the mother. A portrait of him in possession of Mrs. James B. Clay, of Lexington, as described by a member of the family, would more nearly picture to the mind the form, features, and person of the noble dame than would any other object. General Nathaniel W. Watkins resided for many years and until his death with his family, at Morley, Scott County, Missouri. He was the seventh child of Henry and Elizabeth Clay Watkins. We are permitted to quote from a letter of his, written over thirty years ago and not very long before his death, to Clay Taylor, of Pendleton, Warren County, Missouri, a grandson of Reverend Porter Clay:

"I fear I shall not be able to give you much information in relation to your grandfather, Porter Clay. Amongst other losses during the civil war was that of my family register, containing the names, births, and other records of my mother's family.

"Your grandfather was the youngest of the Clay brothers. I can not state the date of his birth. Henry Clay was born, I think, in 1777; Porter a year or two later. He married Sophia Grush, of Maryland, sister to Mrs. Thomas Hart and Mrs. John W. Hunt, of Lexington, Kentucky. She was a most estimable lady. His second wife, you know, was Mrs. Hardin. I came to Missouri in 1820. Prior to that time Porter Clay had become a member of the Baptist Church, and soon after commenced preaching. I never saw him but once after I left Kentucky. He spent a week with me at Jackson, Missouri. He was a warm, zealous, and devoted Christian, and very conscientious in all his duties as such. He devoted the later part of his life to the ministry. He died December 30, 1849, at Camden, Arkansas, where his remains still repose. I am now seventy-eight years old — the sixteenth child of my dear mother — the last of my race surviving. Most of my children are with me."

In a letter to Thomas H. Clay, of Lexington, Kentucky, of date June 22, 1879, Clay Taylor, above mentioned, writes:

"I knew my grandfather, Porter Clay, well. I have often heard him say that he preached the first English sermon ever delivered west of the Mississippi River."

We only learn that John was a "high liver;" that he spent much of his life in New Orleans; there he married Miss Duralde, and finally died in the South. There was no issue of this marriage. Porter Clay followed his father as a minister in the Baptist Church. His chosen field of labor seems to have been Illinois and Missouri, then our western border settlements. We hear of him at Alton, Illinois, in 1848, in the letter to Cassius M. Clay we have copied. He was then past his three score and ten years. Of the sisters we have been able to obtain no certain tracings.

In due course of time after the death of Reverend John Clay, the widow married Henry Watkins, also of Hanover County, Virginia, a gentleman ten years her junior, as before related. Mr. and Mrs. Watkins continued to reside in Virginia after their marriage until

1792, when they moved to Kentucky and settled at the town of Versailles.

We have mentioned that Mary Hudson, the elder sister of Elizabeth, married Captain John Watkins, who was an older brother of Henry, familiarly known as "Hal." Two brothers married the two sisters. Captain John Watkins and family came to Kentucky and settled at Versailles some years in advance of Henry and family. In 1792 he was a delegate in the Constitutional Convention which sat at Danville, and a Representative in the first Legislature, which met at Lexington the same year. On June 23, 1792, the town site of Versailles was established by legislative act on one hundred acres of land, the title of which was vested in John Watkins and six others as Trustees, and John Watkins and Richard Young were appointed commissioners to sell lots and dispose of the proceeds. Henry Watkins and wife, the mother of Henry Clay, followed Captain John and wife to Kentucky.

Whether any of the Clay children came with them we know not certainly. Henry remained in Virginia, attentive to his duties in the clerk's office at Richmond and prosecuting his studies for the law, until 1797, when, in his twenty-first year of age, he also came to Kentucky and located at Lexington. There is little doubt that the removal of his mother, with the Watkins families, to Kentucky determined Henry Clay to locate at Lexington, then the most flourishing city west of the Alleghenies, and there to begin the career which has made his name immortal.

Henry Watkins and wife for some years after settling in Woodford County kept the old hotel stand on Main Street in Versailles, the only hostelry then in the town. It was built of stone by Henry Watkins, on Main Street, on the west side, one square south of the court-house on the same side. The site is now occupied with the bank building of Amsden & Co., which was erected a few years ago. The original structure was of stone, of which a venerable citizen, Mr. Thomas M. Field, says in a letter, "it was a large two-story stone house, the first hotel in Versailles, known as Watkins' Tavern." There was built an annex to this, in time, of wooden frame materials. Within fifteen years past the buildings were destroyed by fire — at least the combustible portions of the same. The old wreck was then removed for the modern structure. There were no hotels in those days of a century ago, at least not in the towns and country, but the tavern stands were famous for over a half century after. They not only accommodated the travel-ing public and private wayfarers, but were the radiating points of the important stage lines which threaded the country in every direction, the headquarters of political leaders who met to caucus and to plan their campaigns, and the general rendezvous for public news and neighborly gossip.   Watkins' Tavern was widely known and somewhat famous as a typical hostelry of the kind described.   No doubt affairs of State and of the nation were discussed in its halls and private chambers ; and by such historic leaders as the Blackburns, the Clays, the Watkinses, and others.   Here LaFayette was entertained when on his tour through Kentucky.

According to the same authority above, Mr. Field, "Henry Watkins, the husband, was an elegant, accomplished gentleman, of good blood and of goodly wealth." Years after they gave up the old tavern stand and settled upon a farm three miles south of Versailles, on the turnpike road leading to Mortonsville.   This property they owned and improved, and here they made their home during the remainder of their lives.   This homestead was opposite what is well known as the "Moss Place."   A number of their kindred and name settled in the country around them.   Mrs. Elizabeth Moss, grandmother of Samuel L. Woolridge, now of Versailles, was a niece of Elizabeth Clay-Watkins and a daughter of Mr. John Watkins, of whom we have made mention before as having married Mary Hudson, the sister of the mother of Henry Clay. Robert McConnell now lives upon the country homestead farm where dwelt and died Henry Watkins and wife. The old residence house has long ago disappeared, and another more modern occupies the ground where it stood. The old landmarks in town and country have passed away with their venerable tenantry, and no pictured relic remains from which we can reproduce their imaged memories on the pages of this book. Mrs. Trabue remembered their residence in the country in the years 1819–29.

For the truest and fullest record of the family of Henry Watkins, after his marriage with the widow Clay and their removal to Kentucky, we are indebted to a letter from R. Cave Graves, Esquire, of Versailles, written in his ninety-first year of age. It was our pleasure to have intimately known this venerable and noble patriarch of the olden days for forty-five years before his death. He entered into his rest a short time after the letter was written in answer to one of our own, and it was perhaps among the last, if not the last, that was penned by fingers trembling with the feebleness of age. It reads as follows :

"VERSAILLES, KENTUCKY, November 13, 1893.

"DEAR FRIEND : I was much gratified in receiving your kind and social letter, and will, as far as able, answer the business portion.

"Mrs. Clay, the mother of Henry, the greatest statesman of his age, came from Virginia in early days and settled in Versailles, Woodford County, with her second husband, Hal Watkins. To them were born four children, three sons and one daughter. The daughter, Patsy, married Colonel William B. Blackburn, a lawyer of Versailles, and uncle to the three brothers, the late Governor Luke; James, the present State Marshal, and our United States Senator, Joe.

"To Colonel Blackburn and wife were born one son, Henry, and one daughter, Henrietta. The daughter was a very interesting and attractive young lady; she married Doctor Flournoy, who died young, leaving one son, David. A few years later Henrietta married a second time, Tom Bartlett, quite a character. To them were born a son, William, and a daughter, Pru, both born blind. Before the children matured the father died, thus leaving the mother of the blind a widow for the second time. Some years after she married a third husband, Frank Holloway, an elegant and good man, who aided his wife in taking care of and providing for the unfortunate son and daughter. David Flournoy, the eldest son of Henrietta spoken of, married Mrs. Sallie Garth, settled in Versailles and died here.

"Of the sons of Elizabeth Clay-Watkins, Frank became a minister of the Baptist Church and stood high with those who knew him. He married at an early day Miss Butler, moved to Missouri and passed out of my sight. John, another son, married Miss Milton and settled in Woodford County. Four children, three sons and one daughter, were born to them. The daughter married a gentleman in Lexington. The children of John live in Fayette County, very independent, and are highly esteemed.

"Henry Blackburn, son of Colonel William and Patsy Watkins Blackburn, married an accomplished young lady, lived here a few years, and finally moved to Rock Island.

"Of Mr. Hal Watkins and his accomplished wife, they were the honor and pride of their neighbors. The visits of her son, Henry Clay, were as certain and regular as the seasons ; and after the death of the accomplished and honored mother, no less attention was paid to his sister, Mrs. Blackburn.

"You will excuse my shaking hand and pencil. You would not expect better things from one traveling on the journey of life, between the ninetieth and ninety-first milestones thereof.

"My kindest regards.

"R. C. GRAVES."

Colonel William B. Blackburn, mentioned in this letter, by marriage to Patsy Watkins became the half-brother-in-law of Henry Clay. His eminence in the law and in politics made his name historic. From the years 1804 to 1838, a lapse of thirty-four years, he served his constituents three sessions in the State Senate and fourteen sessions in the House. In 1828 he was defeated by Robert B. McAfee, as the Anti-Relief candidate for Lieutenant-Governor, in the turbulent and memorable campaign of that period. His relations to the Great Commoner, in politics, by marriage, and as neighbors and friends, were intimate. We doubt not that Mr. Clay found in him one of his ablest supporters.

Mr. T. B. Watkins, grandson of Elizabeth Clay-Watkins, long a merchant of Lexington, Kentucky, of the firm of Spencer & Watkins, in a letter to the author, of date November 9, 1897, says :

"Yours of the 8th instant to hand. In regard to the children of my grandmother by issue of her second marriage, I can not give you a very full account. She had three sons and a daughter to live to a mature age. I have been told several children died in infancy. My father, John Watkins, was the oldest child. He was born in Hanover County, Virginia, in 1785, and died in the State of Missouri in 1845.

"He married Miss Caroline T. Milton, a daughter of Elijah Milton, of this (Fayette) county. They raised ten children, six sons and four daughters. My father was a farmer. Frank Watkins was the next son. I do not know when he was born or when he died. I think he was a farmer. I do not know who he married; he had, I think, four or five children, one of whom was a son. Nathaniel W. Watkins was the youngest child. He was a lawyer by profession. He died in 1866. At the time of his death he was the oldest practitioner of law in this country. He married Miss Eliza Watson, of New Madrid, Missouri. They had seven or eight children. Some of them are now living in Scott County, Missouri. One, I know, lives in Rogers, Arkansas.

"As to my aunt, Patsy Blackburn, you appear to be familiar with her history. She had two children: a son, Henry, and a daughter, Henrietta."

Traditions well agree in their descriptions of the person and character of Elizabeth Clay-Watkins as she was remembered in daily life. Her dark hair and eyes, relieved by a light shading of complexion with a flush of crimson on her cheeks, leaves the impression that she was not distinctly brunette or blonde, as a type of comely womanhood, but perhaps a blending of the two.

She was possessed of strong Anglo-Saxon sense, with great determination of will, and was noted for the orderly industry and thrift with which she conducted her domestic affairs.

The most vivid impressions made upon the mind of the writer of the noble matron were from the reminiscent talk of Mrs. Lucy Trabue, mentioned before. Mrs. Trabue was a fine type of the noble women of Kentucky of the early days of this century.

In her traditional gossip we had the first revelations of the inner life and history of the mother of Henry Clay; and to the notes taken down at the time and preserved is due the inspiration of desire and purpose to gather the materials for the biographic and family sketches of the worthy, but almost forgotten, Daughter of the Revolution who gave to us the immortal Clay.

Mrs. Trabue spoke in terms of admiration, and almost of enthusiasm, of Elizabeth Clay-Watkins. Her description of her personal appearance was very similar to that already given. Her well-rounded and shapely form, indicating great energy and endurance, may have made the impression that she was below the medium in statute. The vigor of mind she displayed was no less manifest than that of body. She unconsciously asserted much of that imperiousness of will which was a distinguishing trait of her illustrious son, and which made him a born leader among men. She was engaging in manners, entertaining in conversation, and a great favorite in social circles. Her individuality was striking and impressive. She was animated and genial in spirit, and readily won the confidence and esteem of others. She spoke with the authority of self-conscious right, yet always with disinterested sympathy in all that concerned her friends. She was not only respected but much reverenced by those who knew her intimately. In her home life she was hospitable and kind to all, and sympathetic and responsive to every call of need among her neighbors. Though somewhat strict in her discipline with her children and servants, she was just and kind, and both paid to her the tribute of obedience with respectful devotion.

The mother of Henry Clay was undoubtedly a woman gifted by nature, and of a marked individuality wrought out in the school of a many-sided life-experience. She was possessed of traits of mind and a force of will and character which made her not only equal to every occasion, but, in emergencies, superior to environment. We reverently honor her memory as the mother of the Great; she was not less one of the heroic women of our country's destiny, in the days of peril when our country needed heroines as well as heroes. Posterity should not do less than remember the deeds of such, and make their names imperishable in our literature and upon the pages of history.

We were able to find a few years ago only two living persons who had been upon familiar visiting terms with Mrs. Clay-Watkins and knew her well in their youth. One was then nearing her eightieth and the other had passed his ninetieth birthday. Both soon after passed away, and we know of no one left to give us other reminiscent traditions on the subject we treat as they knew her in person and life. The honored matron of whom we have written died in 1829, three score and ten years ago, in the eightieth year of her age. Her remains were buried in the country graveyard in the vicinity of the home farm on which she resided at the time of her death, and on the Moss place, near Versailles, in Woodford County, named before. In those early days every neighborhood had a burial-ground where those who died in the vicinity were usually interred. Here her mortal ashes quietly and almost obscurely rested until the year 1851. It was the year preceding the death of the great Henry, her honored son. The burdens of age and of arduous labors in the service of his country lay heavily upon him. The feebler flow of the ebbing tide of life admonished him that the end was not far off. He had calmly made his peace with and committed his soul to God. His thoughts went back, as the thoughts of the aged do, to the memories of childhood and of youthful manhood, of which the image of his mother was a central vision. The lonely isolation of the country graveyard, and the possibility that tablet and epitaph and all vestiges of the inhumed might pass away and fade from record and from memory, came up before his mind. He tenderly cherished the love he bore his mother in her lifetime ; that love was fresh in memory since her death. He determined to have her remains removed and deposited in his family lot in the Lexington Cemetery, where, with other loved ones of his household, they might sleep side by side with his own. The venerable warder of this City of the Dead, C. S. Bell, tells yet in graphic words how he received directions from Mr. Clay, nearing a half century ago, to remove and re-inter the remains of his mother in the spot where they yet rest, *Lot Number Thirty-seven, Section I.* It is located nearly due west of and about two hundred yards from the Clay monument.

The monument ordered by Henry Clay for his mother's grave is of pure Italian marble. It stands nine feet in height from the ground, in somewhat massive yet symmetric proportions, and was artistically fashioned and erected by Pruden, of Lexington, in the year of re-interment, 1851. Around it are grouped a number of the graves of the descendants of Henry and Lucretia Hart Clay, the stones and their epitaphs marking the spots of their sepulture. But the ashes of the Great Commoner do not repose at this family consecrated spot, as he anticipated. He belonged to the people in life, and the people claimed, in the name of the whole country, the privilege of paying such obsequies to his mortal remains as befitted the name of the Great Commoner, written, as it is, in imperishable lines in the memories and hearts of his countrymen. The dust of the immortal dead lies sacredly sealed in the sarcophagus which rests in the vault within the base of the towering Clay monument.

We copy the inscriptive words as composed by her immortal son and carved in the marble which marks the place where rest the remains of the sainted and beloved mother:

ELIZABETH WATKINS,

FORMERLY

ELIZABETH CLAY;

BORN, 1750.

DIED, 1829.

THIS MONUMENT, A TRIBUTE TO HER MANY DOMESTIC VIRTUES, HAS BEEN PROMPTED BY THE FILIAL AFFECTION AND VENERATION OF ONE OF HER GRATEFUL SONS,

H. CLAY.

The most commanding eminence in the cemetery grounds was selected for the site of this monument, and from the pinnacle of the lofty shaft the statue of Henry Clay overlooks every object and scene within the sacred City of the Dead and in the city and country in view.

The Clay family is one of the most remarkable that our country has produced. It has become historic in national and State affairs, through representative members who have held positions of official eminence and who have distinguished the name in public life. Biographers and historians have dwelt upon their careers and achievements, and have made their names as familiar as household words to the people of our own country and abroad. Beyond mention of these, the public has known, or has had opportunity to know, little of the types of manhood and womanhood of the numerous posterity from the ranks of which these distinguished men have sprung. For nearly three hundred years, since the emigration of the first ancestor from England, and for ten generations, the Clays have figured in American life, in public and in private affairs, as prominently and as potentially perhaps as any family within our national realm. The qualities of hereditary virile manhood displayed in public life by those members of the family whose names have become historic are well known. One acquainted with descendants of the several branches, in private life, will be impressed with a sameness of qualities in all. The individualities by which we discriminate the variety or type of character traits are marked. The impressions formed of the historic members of the Clays — their high order of intelligence, their courage and loyalty of conviction, and their boldness of sentiment and independence of will — we find confirmed in the more private ranks of the numerous kindred wherever found. The brilliancy and power of Henry Clay as orator, statesman, and diplomat, and his masterly creation and leadership of a great national party for a generation, were peerless; yet many, who saw little below the display of genius, believed him superficial, because they were themselves superficial. The far-sighted sagacity, the boldness and daring of Cassius M. Clay, as the open leader of anti-slavery reform in the midst of fortressed pro-slaveryism in Kentucky, led many to look upon him as a visionary and reckless agitator. Many can now see that he was but a generation in advance of the sentiment of his day. Beneath this display of genius and originality upon the surface there is a foundation of solid and enduring qualities to be found in all branches of the family, in public or in private life. Within our State there are hundreds of the posterity of Henry Clay of the third generation in America, the common ancestor of all the Clays in Kentucky.

They are more numerously settled in Bourbon, Fayette, and Madison counties than elsewhere, just where the three immigrant ancestors planted the first stock a century or so ago. A chief trait of character is the love of home and of the life of domesticity; with rare exceptions, the Clays are instinctive home-builders and home-stayers. Another trait is a predilection to acquire lands and to hold them tenaciously. It is safe to say that there is no other old Kentucky family that can compare with the Clay posterity in the number, the quality, and the value of fine landed estates owned. Among these are many magnificent bluegrass farms in the highest state for tillage and stock-raising. On these are the country mansion homes of the owners, with every appurtenance for comfort and convenience. The Clays are good livers of the old Kentucky style, and hospitality and good cheer are dispensed in the old Kentucky way. We have men--tioned the incident that the home sites of the three ancestors of the Kentucky families, selected for settlement a century or more ago, are yet held by descendants. Cassius M. Clay, nearing his ninetieth birthday, resides at the home-place of his father, General Green Clay, over one hundred years ago, in Madison County, in a magnificent mansion costing eighty thousand dollars, situated upon a tract of more than one thousand acres of fertile land. The descendants of Henry Clay to-day own Ashland, near Lexington, and live royally there. A great-grandson of Doctor Henry Clay, of Bourbon County, dwells not less sumptuously at the old homestead site located one hundred and ten years ago when a stockade fort was needed to protect the first settler against savage foes. The coincidence illustrates the solid and enduring qualities which distinguish the family type of character. The numerous posterity are represented, not only in public life and upon the farm, but in all honorable avocations; they have shown themselves worthy of an illustrious and virtuous ancestry. The Hudson family into which the father of Henry Clay married has furnished no members who were known all over the civilized world as statesmen and orators, but it has supplied representatives with heads full of sound sense and hearts full of sterling virtues. The father of the mother of Henry Clay could stand in the front door of his colonial mansion and look out upon broad acres well stocked and cultivated which were his own. He had plenty of slaves to work his lands and to wait upon himself and his family. He feared no visit from the sheriff to deprive him of his lands or his slaves for debts, because he owed no one what he could not pay.

The will of George Hudson was made and signed

in the year 1770. In its provisions he bequeathed to his children and grandchildren thirty-one slaves, each by name, together with their issue. Besides the home plantation upon which he had resided, which contained nearly five hundred acres of land, there were other lands and personal property devised. Altogether these properties made up an estate ample to justify a style of living such as the best families of Virginia in that day were accustomed to enjoy.

At the date of this will, 1770, three children had been born to Reverend John and Elizabeth Clay, and were living — Betsy Hudson Clay, George Hudson Clay, and Henry Clay (the first Henry) — to each of whom by name the grandfather bequeathed a negro. Born in 1750, Elizabeth Clay was then but twenty years old, yet the mother of three children. We infer from these incidents mentioned that she married young — perhaps when but fifteen years of age.

In 1780 was made and signed the will of Reverend John Clay, ten years after that of George Hudson. The names of two out of three of the Clay children mentioned in the grandfather's will, Betsy Hudson Clay and Henry Clay, are omitted in the provisions of that of the father. These two meanwhile had died. We finally lose trace of the other children mentioned, except John, Henry, and

Porter, who only, as far as we know, lived to full maturity and died in advanced age.

John Clay disposed of twenty-one slaves by name, to be distributed among his widow and children, in this instrument. There were "other negroes not mentioned above," to go to the children as the law provided; how many we do not know. By the will of George Hudson, sixteen negroes were made over to Mrs. John Clay and children, "with their increase" for ten years. It is very probable that John and Elizabeth Clay were possessed at this time of at least thirty slaves. He further disposed of his plantation "at Euphraim," in Henrico County, from which he had removed in 1777, with his family, to the Hudson plantation in Hanover County. He provided also for the sale or distribution of personal property, and finally devised the homestead plantation on which they then resided. Such an estate of land, slaves, and personal property as was owned and in possession at the time of the demise of Reverend John Clay, when his son Henry was four years old, furnished the resources not only for a competency but for living in the style of the English gentry of that period. Among so many servants there could have been no lack of laborers to till the fields and do the heavy work of the farm; there could have been no lack of female labor to do the household work, and to spin and weave and sew; and these things done, would leave a half-dozen or more pickaninnies to run errands, nurse or play with the white children, and do chores about the premises. What may have happened, besides the death of John Clay, to have disturbed this happiest relation of capital and labor, and to have reduced in circumstances this Clay family, we may not know in all. We suspect, however, that a number of the valuable field hands were among the negroes abducted by Tarleton's troopers very soon after, and that the productive capacity of the plantations was seriously impaired by the untimely visit of the marauders. John Clay's health failing soon after he had purchased of John Watkins and wife their half-interest in the Hudson home plantation, the purchase money was not yet paid; nor was it to be due until one year after the death of Mrs. George Hudson, who made her home with and was being cared for by her daughter, Mrs. John Clay. She died in 1781, in the same year with John Clay. This seems to have been a year of sore trials and heavy sorrows in the household. In the midst of many heart-crushing bereavements and burdens, Tarleton's bandit-troopers sacked and plundered her house, and carried off a number of her most reliant laboring men. It was a *dies iræ* in the stricken home.

The main pillar of the domestic temple fell away when Reverend John Clay died. Had he lived in health, with two plantations and thirty slaves, he should have supported his family in comfort and competence. But death came amid the disorders and disasters of cruel war, then widowhood and orphanage, then division of property, then litigation of years in the courts, then the breaking of the home-circle and the parting of mother and children, and finally the exodus to Kentucky, then the Land of Promise. Henry Clay was fifteen years of age when his mother removed to Kentucky in 1792. He had been educated in the country schools until this event, when he took a position as salesman and clerk in a retail store in Richmond. At this time he says of himself: "Being left now without guardian, without pecuniary means of support, to steer my course as I might or could." From this modest beginning he was, a year or so after, taken into the office of Peter Tinsley, then clerk of the High Court of Chancery of Virginia. This fortunate incident shaped the future of the Great Commoner. The school of experience was his best master.

But the strangest episode amid the solemnities of will-making, of death and obsequies, and of widowhood and tears of this dramatic period and its scenes was the serene and confident manner with which Reverend John

7

Clay took for granted that his widow soon to be would
marry again: ''Except my loving wife should intermarry
betwixt this and then." The proviso comes in more than
once. In the eyes of her gallant and devoted husband
Mrs. Clay must yet have been a very comely and a very
attractive woman. They had been married fifteen or
sixteen years, and she had borne him nine children.
In this our day the two conditions would be assumed
an almost insuperable bar to a second marriage. Such
an event might happen yet, but the probability would be
so remote that no man would likely, in writing his will,
anticipate the event with so much seriousness at this end
of the Nineteenth Century. But John Clay was fore-
sighted and correct in the estimate he placed on the
beauty and attractiveness of his matronly wife. The
Widow Clay not only married again in due time, but
married ''an elegant and accomplished gentleman," as
related by one who should know — a gentleman but
twenty-three years of age and ten years her junior.
Mrs. Clay was not only a most marriageable lady, but
she lived in a marriageable age. The marital union
in both instances proved happy in results and fruitful
enough in an age when parents delighted to believe with
the Psalmist, that ''Children are a heritage of the Lord;
as arrows are in the hands of a mighty man, so are

children of the youth; happy is the man that hath his quiver full of them." Nine children were the issue of the first marriage to Reverend John Clay, and seven were afterward born to Henry and Elizabeth Clay-Watkins. We quote again from the letter of Nathaniel W. Watkins, of Morley, Missouri, the half-brother of Henry Clay: "I am the sixteenth child of my dear mother — the last of my race surviving" — an instance of motherhood which may tax the credulity of some of our modern day. But large families of children were the rule then, not the exception. It was thus that our grand, and great-grand, and great-great-grandparents peopled Kentucky from Virginia, and from Kentucky peopled Illinois and Missouri and Arkansas, and finally the Great West. It is part of our history to be proud of.

The will of John Clay was as wisely and equitably ordered as a devoted and justice-loving husband and father could have framed it, so far as we can judge from its perusal. It provides that his estate shall remain intact until his eldest son, George, shall reach the age of twenty years, unless the widow should intermarry again, and associates two friendly neighbors with his wife as executors. George, the second child, was born about 1768; he would have reached his twentieth birthday in 1788. The provisions would give to each child its portion when of an age to launch out into self-sustaining life : the sons at twenty, the daughters at eighteen. The will contemplated preserving the family unity under the mother's care until each was of mature age, and as long after as it might be deemed best to remain under the home-roof by any of the children, in the event the widow and mother remained unmarried. These conditions might have made a happy household of all, barring the shadows of sorrowful memories of the past; and few such households are without such shadows. But in the event of a second marriage, the provisions of the will gave to the widow a lifetime interest in the plantation, in which his title seems to have been perfect, and enough slaves to till the same and for domestic service. This should have secured her the comforts of a good home for her lifetime, with industrious and prudent care on the part of her second husband. The second husband, however, and the second set of children had no interest in this remainder of the estate after the death of the wife and mother, Elizabeth Clay-Watkins. Such a future was not promising to them; therefore Henry Watkins turned his eye toward Kentucky, the refuge of all in Virginia who then sought to better fortune. What disposition was made before their emigration of the life interest in the Henrico plantation and slaves we have no certain record.

We indulge just a little curiosity in the fate of some obscure members of the old Clay household. In the will of John Clay he devised to his sons several negroes by name : Daniel and Arthur to John Clay; James and Little Sam to Henry Clay, and Dick and Harry to Porter Clay. What became of Daniel and Arthur, of James and Little Sam, of Dick and Harry in the dispersion from the happy home of childhood? If we were familiar with the inner life and scenes of this little Southern domestic realm of the good days of long - ago, we would find a pathos of sentiment in this allotment of negroes. There were doubtless some associations and ties formed in the infancy and boyhood of these servants and their new young masters which suggested the devisement in each instance. Those who were reared in such Southern homes in the *ante - bellum* period can imagine the relations. The nurses in infancy became guardian companions in later years. The negro boys of twelve and fifteen years of age romped and played and laughed and prattled with the white children of three and four and six years. It is most probable that James or Little Sam, or both, were such companions of four - year-old Henry Clay. If so, we may be assured that, when the orchard and garden were invaded, little Henry got a full share of the best apples or peaches or cherries from the top limbs, or of the ripest berries or melons that grew on the vines. In turn, Henry and his brothers just as surely begged many a holiday for the negroes, which they spent together fishing and larking along the banks of Mechump's Creek, or hunting pawpaws and hickory nuts in the forest of the Hanover plantation. If a partridge nest full of eggs was found, or a young squirrel was caught, the greatest pleasure in the prize was the delight it would give to the "chil'len at the house." What became of James and Little Sam? The lips that once could tell are sealed now, and the story of their simple lives, linked with the child-life of the immortal Clay as they were, is lost forever.

It is not a little remarkable that the court records of Hanover County, Virginia, and the judges refer to the deceased father of Henry Clay as Sir John Clay. There is a family tradition that Henry Clay, when asked for an explanation of this entitlement, would answer with a light laugh, and waive further discussion by saying that he thought it was but a soubriquet bestowed upon his father. In the court proceedings, however, the title is given with a seriousness of formality that lends it an importance beyond that of a mere soubriquet. The courts paid far more respect in those days to phrases and forms of pleadings than they do now. A misnomer of plaintiff or defendant might be a ground of nonsuit, or a miscarriage of the case. In the bill filed in the answers of John Watkins, of Henry Watkins, and of Augustine Easton, and in the decree of the Court, the address of Sir John Clay is uniformly used. We can only infer that the subject was Sir John Clay, in the eye of law and under the forms of Court proceedings; that simple John Clay would not have been sufficient identification. Finally, we curiously inquire, if the subject was not Sir John Clay, why, in this serious connection, give the title? We can readily see why Reverend John Clay might modestly omit the title in writing or using his name in his ordinary business transactions.

We have mentioned before that the three immigrant ancestors of the Clay posterities in Kentucky, General Green Clay, Colonel Henry Clay, of Bourbon County, and Henry Clay, of Lexington, are descendants of Sir John Clay, of Wales, England. The father of John Clay and grandfather of Henry Clay was John Clay, senior. The father of John Clay, senior, was Henry Clay; his father was Charles Clay; and his father was Captain John Clay, the son of Sir John, of Wales. Captain John came to America in 1613, and settled at or near Jamestown, in Virginia. From this first American ancestor, through his son Charles and his grandson Henry, are descended all the Clays of Kentucky. General Green Clay, Doctor Henry Clay, and Reverend John Clay were sons of brothers, and first cousins. Henry Clay, Colonel Henry Clay, of Bourbon, and Cassius M. and Brutus Clay were second cousins.

Very naturally we infer that in some way the title Sir John Clay here conferred on the father of Henry Clay was connected with his descent from the remote ancestor, Sir John Clay, of Wales. The Federal Constitution was not yet adopted, and Virginia was in the chaotic period of transition from colonial government to full-fledged statehood. The proceedings of the courts were yet under the institutions and the usage largely of the English rule. The law of primogeniture, if no longer in force in fact, might yet sometimes be observed in form. Was John Clay the eldest son of eldest sons, back to his ancestor, Sir John, of Wales? This question may be more fittingly answered in the records of genealogy.

Before the old colonial regime gave way to the leveling influences of democracy and popular suffrage, titles of nobility and other class distinctions were worn in Virginia and respected by all, without question or offense, as in the mother country. In the court records of Hanover County it may be seen, when the will of John Clay was presented for record, it was proven by "the oaths of John Stark, Gentleman, and of Isaac Perrin, witnesses thereto." The clerk of the court took for granted that Isaac Perrin was not a gentleman, and said so, virtually, by attaching gentleman to Stark's name and omitting it from Perrin's. Such distinctions were common in those days in Virginia, and in Kentucky also. What Isaac Perrin accepted with equanimity then, if applied now, would be sufficient cause to start a vendetta. Gentlemen and ladies are as plentiful now in our country as people, "without regard to race, color, or condition." The political pie-hunters and hand-shakers have obliterated class distinctions under the favoring providence of democratic institutions.

By intermarriage of George Hudson with Elizabeth Jennings the descendants of these were classed among the numerous heirs to the notorious Jennings estate supposed to be in England; also to the reported Cary estate. From a letter of Edwin Farrar, of Virginia, to Honorable James B. Clay, we are permitted to quote:

"RICHMOND, VIRGINIA, September 7, 1852.

". . . In regard to the Jennings estate, our family are entitled to a share through Mr. Charles Hudson, who died in Hanover in 1745; and your father's claim is through Mr. George Hudson, who was Inspector of Tobacco in Hanover town. He was your father's (maternal) grandfather. They both, I am satisfied, married Jennings; and the Jennings married with the

Carys. So, we are equally interested in the Cary estate, estimated to be worth $250,000,000; while the Jennings estate amounts to $78,000,000. Mr. Abraham requires a power of attorney from all the legatees and also about $8,000 to go to England, and he wants every thing fixed by the first of October."

No doubt Mr. Abraham induced a goodly number of legatees to contribute, and thus to pay the expenses of a trip to Europe. But Mr. James B. Clay, like his father, had but little confidence in the myth of a Jennings or a Cary estate, and declined to contribute to the scheme of investigation and for the benefit of its promotion. Mr. Farrar, however, continues, and makes mention of some family history of the Hudsons:

"Your father (Henry Clay) wrote me a letter in December, 1851, from Washington, giving me somewhat of a history of his family. He said that when he was a small boy his mother and his mother's sister used to go and stay with Aunt Jennings in Louisa County, adjoining Hanover. Also, that he thought that his family and ours, the Hudson family, were connected with the Jennings. Mr. Charles Hudson, in his will in 1745, speaks of Elizabeth Jennings and Ro. Jennings, all of whom lived in Hanover."

Another coincidence in the trend of sentiment common to the Clay ancestors of Kentucky is found in their open and avowed advocacy of emancipation, with a view to a riddance of slavery. In the campaign preceding the adoption of the Second Constitution of Kentucky in 1800, Henry Clay openly and boldly pleaded for a provision in the instrument looking to such end. Though he jeopardized his popularity after in the Southern States, he steadily held to these views, and warned the country of the dangers in the future that threatened a perpetuation of slavery. He originated and organized "The American Emancipation and Colonization Society" at Washington, D. C., as a possible measure of partial relief from the evils foreseen. The original draft of the constitution of this society, in Mr. Clay's own writing, by a rare incident fell into the hands of the author some years ago. The chaste and beautiful chirography of the great orator and statesman was unmistakable in the manuscript, though faded by the lapse of many years.

The bold and daring advocacy of emancipation in the campaign preceding the Constitution of Kentucky of 1850, by Cassius M. Clay, was among the most dramatic episodes of our State history. Only those who lived here in that day and were old enough to observe and remember can appreciate the intensity and proscriptiveness of the pro-slavery sentiment, even in Kentucky. It brooked no public contention or question of slave-rights save at the peril of person or life. Yet in the face of such peril Cassius M. Clay defied the tyranny of opinion that would have sealed his lips, sent his appointments from town to town, and asserted the freedom of speech. There was no other man in America who had the courage and nerve to have made such a campaign. It is needless to say the events were tragic as well as dramatic. He came out with his life ; that was all, and more than could be said of all opponents. Henry Clay and Cassius M. Clay were political seers with the highest order of statesmanship that looked far into the future and read between the lines of Southern doctrinairism and warned of the inevitable catastrophe that must follow the continuance of slavery in our republic. Both had these high convictions and were brave enough to assert them.

We are indebted to Miss Lucretia Hart Clay, of Lexington, Kentucky, for a copy of the record of a friendly suit in the High Court of Chancery of Virginia, brought for the purpose of settling the estates of the Reverend John Clay and George Hudson, and perfecting the title to certain real estate once owned by them. In this record are preserved the wills of George Hudson and Reverend John Clay, and the decree of the court granting the prayer of the petitioners. These wills can hardly fail to be of interest to the numerous descendants of the Clays and Hudsons and Watkinses, as well as to many not related to them by blood or marriage. In this article we have had occasion more than once to refer to these wills and this decree of the court, and we now give them in full, just as they appear in the record:

THE WILL OF GEORGE HUDSON.

In the Name of God, Amen.

I, George Hudson, of Hanover County, do make and ordain this to be my last Will and Testament in manner and form following, to wit:

Imprimis.   I lend to my loving wife, Elizabeth Hudson, eleven negroes, Charles, Anny, Betty, India, Sabray, Mary, John, Jones, Una, Aaron, and Cæsar, also my riding chair and harness, and what household furniture she shall think necessary. All these things I lend her during her natural life, and after her decease I give and bequeath four of the above negroes, viz: Betty, Mary, Anny, and Una, with their future increase, to my daughter Mary Watkins, to her and her heirs forever. And four more of the said negroes, viz: Charles, Sabray, Judy, and Cæsar, with their future increase, I give to my daughter Elizabeth Clay, to her and her heirs forever; and the remaining three I desire may be equally divided, they and their increase, between my two daughters, Mary Watkins and Elizabeth Clay, they and their heirs forever.

Item.   I give unto my daughter, Mary Watkins, the following negroes, viz: Nancy, Sarah, Bersheba, Betty, and Dorum, already in her possession; also Will, Sue, and Mollie, with their future increase, to her and her heirs forever.

Item.   I give unto my daughter, Elizabeth Clay, the following negroes, viz: Polly, Hannah, Bob, and Frank, already in her possession; also Lucy, Farey, and Little Lucy, with their future increase, to her and her heirs forever.

Item. I give to my granddaughter, Betsy Hudson Clay, one negro girl named Rachael, to her and her heirs forever.

Item. I give to my grandson, Henry Clay, one negro boy, Ben, to him and his heirs forever.

Item. I give to my grandson, George Hudson Clay, one negro boy named Bob, to him and his heirs forever.

Item. I give unto my granddaughter, Betsy Jennings Watkins, a negro girl named Aggie, with her increase, to her heirs forever.

Item. I give unto my grandson, Hudson Watkins, one negro boy named Ben, to him and his heirs forever.

My will and desire is that my wife may have the use of the plantation whereon I formerly lived, during her life, and after her death to be sold at the discretion of my executors, and the money arising from same be equally divided between my two daughters, Mary Watkins and Elizabeth Clay; and I desire all other lands that I am possessed with at my death, be sold and divided between my two daughters; and my will and desire is that my wife shall have the benefit of the interest of one third of the money arising from such sale, and all the residue and remainder of my estate, not before mentioned or given away, I desire may be sold and the money equally divided between my two children, Mary Watkins and Elizabeth Clay. I desire my estate may not be appraised, and I will that if either of the legatees or their heirs shall be dissatisfied with what I have thought fit to give them, so as to go to law or make any disturbance, that they or either of them shall not be entitled to any thing which I have thought fit to leave them. Lastly, I do appoint and ordain my wife, Elizabeth, executrix, and my son-in-law, John Watkins, executor, to this my last will and testament.

Revoking all former wills made by me, and declaring this to be my last will and testament.

In witness whereof I have hereunto set my hand and seal, this 30th November, in the year of our Lord, 1770.

GEORGE HUDSON.

Witnesses: THOMAS TINSLEY,
THOMAS CLARKE,
THOMAS OLIVER.

At a court held for Hanover County, Thursday, 14th day of April, 1773, this last will and testament of George Hudson, deceased, was offered to proof at last court by Elizabeth Hudson and John Watkins, executors therein named, and proved by the oath of Thomas Tinsley and Thomas Clarke, two of the witnesses thereto, and ordered to be recorded.

WM. POLLARD, C. H. C.

THE WILL OF REVEREND JOHN CLAY.

IN THE NAME OF GOD, AMEN:

I, John Clay, of Hanover County, being very sick and weak, but of disposing mind and sound memory, do make and ordain this to be my last will and testament, in manner and form following: Imprimis: First of all I recommend my soul to God, who gave it, hoping that through the mediation and sufferings of my Lord and Saviour, to receive free pardon of all my sins, and my body to be decently buried at the direction of my executor, hereafter mentioned.

Item. I desire my stock of horses and cattle may be sold and all my just debts be paid. Item: My will and desire is that all estate, real and personal, be kept together until my eldest son, George Clay, shall arrive at the age of twenty years old, except my loving wife should intermarry betwixt this and then. If she should marry, then in that case I desire all my estate, real and personal, may be delivered up to my executors, except such part as I shall hereafter mention for her use.

Item. I lend to my loving wife, Elizabeth Clay, after my son arrives to the age above mentioned, or the time she does intermarry, if before, the use of my plantation at Euphraim, in Henrico County, together with seven negroes, Charles, India, Cæsar, left her by father's will, Sam, Paul, Chester, Bob, and Fanny during her natural life, and also two feather beds and furniture; also a child's part of stock that may be at the time she marries, or my son comes to the age above mentioned; and after her decease, all the above lent to be sold and equally divided among all my children alive that day, and to their heirs forever.

Item. I give and bequeath to my son, George Clay, three negroes, to wit: Hanover, Bob, and Ben, to him and his heirs forever.

Item. I give and bequeath to my daughter, Salley Clay, two negroes, to wit : Sue and Frank, to her and her heirs forever.

Item. I give and bequeath to my daughter, Molly Clay, two negroes, to wit : Annaca and Little India, to her and her heirs forever.

Item. I give and bequeath to my son, John Clay, two negroes, to wit : Daniel and Arthur, to him and his heirs forever.

Item. I give and bequeath to my son, Henry Clay, two negroes, to wit : James and Little Sam, to him and his heirs forever.

Item. I give and bequeath to my son, Porter Clay, to wit : Dick and Harry, to him and his heirs forever.

Item. I give and bequeath to my child my wife is now pregnant with, if it should live, equal with my other children, out of my other negroes not mentioned above, to its heirs and assigns forever.

Item. My will and desire is that all the rest of my estate shall be equally divided amongst all my children, and if any should die before they arrive, the males to the age of twenty years, and the females, if not married, at the age of eighteen years, that then their part shall be equally divided amongst the surviving children, and if any of my children should lose any of their negroes above mentioned in their lots, that then such loss is to be made good out of my estate to them and their heirs forever.

Item. My will and desire is that the land I now live on, or any part thereof, may not be sold until my son, George Clay, arrives at the age herein mentioned, or until my wife intermarries; that then it may be sold by my executors, and the money arising from the sale be equally disposed of among my sons, or to be laid out in land at their discretion, and be equally divided amongst my sons as they come to the age of twenty years, to them and their heirs forever.

Item. I desire my estate may not be appraised, and do appoint my loving wife, Elizabeth Clay, my executrix, and Colonel Nathaniel Wilkerson and Mr. Richard Chapman executors of this my last will and testament, revoking all other wills heretofore made.

In witness whereof I have hereunto set my hand and seal, this 4th day of November, 1780.

JOHN CLAY.

Signed, sealed, and published in the presence of

JOHN STARK, SENIOR,
CHARLES WINGFIELD,
ISAAC PERRIN,
CHARLES BRIDGWATER.

At a court held for Hanover County, Thursday, seventh day of February, 1782, this last will and testament of John Clay was offered for proof by Richard Chapman, an executor therein named, and was proved by the oath of John Stark, Gentleman, and Isaac Perrin, Witnesses thereto, and also by the oath of the said executor, and was ordered to be recorded.

A copy.

WILLIAM POLLARD, JUNIOR, C. H. C.

ROBERT POLLARD,

FOR WILLIAM POLLARD, JUNIOR, C. H. C.

THE DECREE OF THE COURT.

This cause was this day fully heard upon the bill, answer, and exhibits, and the argument of counsel on both sides, on consideration whereof the court is of opinion that the lands devised in the will of George Hudson, to be sold and the money divided between his two daughters, Mary Watkins and Elizabeth Clay, is to be considered as money subject to disposition of their husbands, John Watkins and Sir John Clay, who might and did elect to have such money raised by the sale of the lands in the lifetime of Elizabeth Hudson, the testator's widow, so as not to disturb her possession or interest therein.

That the sale made by John Watkins, executor (and proprietor of the moiety of the money), to Sir John Clay, in the proceedings mentioned, though not carried into complete execution, was a fair agreement and ought to be established; and was, on the part of the said Sir John, a disposition of his wife's share of the money. Therefore it is decreed and ordered that the complainants, executors of the will of the said Sir John Clay, do, pursuant to his will, sell the lands in the bill mentioned at public sale for ready money, so far as the amount of the money hereinafter mentioned as due to John Watkins, and the residue on six months' credit, previously advertising the time and place of such sale for three weeks in one of the Virginia Gazettes, out of the money arising by such sale, do pay to the defendant, John Watkins, and Mary, his wife, three hundred and twenty-five pounds and interest money thereon from the end of the year from the time of the death of Elizabeth Hudson till paid, and dispose of the residue of the purchase money after deducting the expense of sale and the costs of this suit, according to the will of said Clay. That the said complainants with John Watkins and Mary, his wife, and Henry Watkins and Elizabeth, his wife, do join in a conveyance of the said land to the purchaser in fee-simple, and the complainants are to return an account of sales to this court to be registered herein.

A true copy of the record.

WM. W. HERRIND, C. S. C. C. R. D.

PERSONAL.

We have had to gather up the materials for this work from varied sources, and by researches extending through several years. Besides the invaluable contributions which are mentioned fully, from Mrs. Lucy Trabue, R. C. Graves, Esquire, and Thomas B. Watkins, we acknowledge indebtedness to Mrs. Josephine Henry, who was among the first to take interest in the correspondence ; to Mrs. James B. Clay and to Miss Lucretia Hart Clay, who have furnished largely the documents and information needed ; to Mr. E. F. Clay and Judge H. Clay Howard, of Paris ; to Mr. Thomas H. Clay, of Lexington ; to the venerable warden of the cemetery, Mr. C. S. Bell, and to others who have added more or less to the materials from which this paper has been prepared. The subject proper of the history and genealogy of the Clay family in America the writer most cheerfully leaves for treatment in another department by the very able pen of Mrs. Mary Rogers Clay. The name and accomplishments of Mrs. Clay are familiar to all who know her as the editor of the genealogical columns of the Courier-Journal in recent years. With unremitting industry and critical care she has gathered the data for her work to follow. From such an able source it can not fail to be an interesting and valuable contribution to the personal and family history of our country and to the literature which belongs to it.

Mrs. MARY ROGERS CLAY.

PART SECOND

The Genealogy of the Clays

BY

Mrs. Mary Rogers Clay

Member of The Filson Club

THE GENEALOGY OF THE CLAYS.

"There may be and there often is a regard for ancestry which nourishes a weak pride, but there is also a moral and philosophical respect for our ancestors which elevates the character and improves the heart."— *Daniel Webster.*

In "Hotten's List of Emigrants to America, 1600–1700," we find among the "MUSTERS OF THE INHABITANTS OF VIRGINIA" these items:

"The MUSTER of the Inhabitant's of Jordans Journey, Charles Cittie, taken the 21th, of January 1624." Of these:

"The Muster of John Claye.

JOHN CLAYE arrived in the TREASUROR, February, 1613.
ANNE, his wife, in the Ann, August, 1623.

Servant.

William Nicholls aged 26 yeres, in the Dutie, in May, 1619."

THIS is the first mention of the name in colonial records. At this period of Virginia history Sir Thomas Dale was Governor, and, having been bred a soldier, ruled with great severity. He was so harsh the people hated him. He punished men by flogging and by setting them to work in irons for years. Those who rebelled or ran away were put to death in cruel ways: some were burned alive, others were broken on the wheel, and one man, for merely stealing food, was starved to death ; yet the colony prospered under his administration. He abolished the ''common store'' system, declaring it was a premium for idleness, just suited for the drones who would not work, knowing that, however the harvest prospered, the general store must maintain them. Each man was granted a home and three acres of land, which he himself must cultivate, paying therefor two and a half barrels of corn to the public granary. These allotments of lands were gradually increased, and finally Governor Dale persuaded the London Company to grant fifty acres in fee-simple to each colonist who would clear and cultivate them and pay annually a nominal rent to the King ''at the feast of St. Michael the Archangel.'' Those paying into the treasury the sum of twelve pounds and ten shillings should be entitled to one hundred acres, to be located as desired. From this allotment there gradually grew up along the James River and some of its tributaries a settled though scattered community of planters dependent upon their own exertions for support and free from the evil associations and vices engendered in the earlier days of Jamestown.

Of this class was Captain John Clay, ''the English Grenadier,'' of whom we have so many traditions. He was living in Charles City in 1624.

"Patent (210) grants John Clay twelve hundred acres in Charles City County, Virginia, beginning at the lands granted by order of Court to Francis Hooke, up to the head of Ward's, his creek, and bounded on the north by James River. Due one hundred acres to him as an old planter before the government of Sir Thomas Dale, and the other eleven hundred for the transportation of twenty-two persons by the "West," July 13, 1635." (Ledger I, page 230.)

"These lands granted John Clay were near the present City Point, only a few miles from what is now Chesterfield County, and no other settler of the name is mentioned in any record in this section."—*Richmond Critic, 1888.*

---

1. Captain Clay had been married before leaving England, and left his wife behind. He probably sent for her as soon as he had prepared a comfortable home. Why he delayed so long, those familiar with the history of the Jamestown Colony best understand. Hunger, despair, and death followed the one so fast in the wake of the other that twice within a few years that colony was reduced from five hundred persons to less than sixty souls, and in 1616 there were only three hundred and fifty English people in all North America.

The children of Captain John and Ann Clay, so far as known, were :

> I. Francis Clay, whose name appears on the records of Northumberland County, Virginia, from October 19, 1652, in the grants of lands, until June 8, 1658, and in Westmoreland County on May 21, 1666.

II. WILLIAM CLAY. In 1655 William Bayley had a patent for four
hundred acres of land on Ward's Creek, purchased of William Clay, son of John Clay, assignee of Francis Hooke,
patentee of 1637.

III. THOMAS CLAY, one of fourteen persons "who did unlawfully
Assemble at ye pish church o Lawnes Creeke, with Intent to
declare they would not pay theire publiq taxes, & yt they
expected diverse others to meet them. (Surry Co., 3rd Jany
Ao. Dom. 1673.)" (William and Mary Quarterly Magazine.)

2. IV. CHARLES CLAY, born 1638, died 1686 (intestate). He married
Hannah Wilson, daughter of John Wilson, senior, of Henrico County, Virginia, and states in Court, April, 1686,
that he has received his wife's part of her father's estate.
(1688 – 1697, page 360.)

2. Charles Clay was a soldier in the "Great Rebellion
of 1676;" one of those "good housekeepers, well-armed"
that followed the gallant Bacon in his effort to free Virginia. Of this service the family traditions are fully verified by the records of the Henrico Court. Depositions
are there regarding the confiscation and killing of cattle
by General Bacon's soldiers. In this list is the name of
Charles Clay. (Bk. 1677–92.) We know he was a gallant soldier, for his worthy descendants have been such
wherever they have fought, whether at Ninety - Six, New
Orleans, Buena Vista, Chickamauga, or Santiago; yet we
wonder (is it disloyal to wonder?) if he were one of the
rebels at work on the breastworks in front of the pali-
sades that bright September night when Madam Bray,
Madam Page, Madam Ballard, the "white - apron" guard,
sat in the forefront?

Hannah (Wilson) Clay was granted administration on the estate of Charles Clay by order of Court, June 1, 1686. (Bk. 1677–1692, page 368.)

Charles Clay's estate was settled and debts paid by Hannah Clay, October 12, 1688. (Bk. 1688–1697, page 8.)

Extracts from the inventory and appraisement of the estate of Charles Clay, deceased, presented June 15, 1686, by Hannah Clay, administratrix :

Cows &c, belonging to Mary Clay, one of ye orphans, which were given her by her God-father.

Cows &c belonging to Elizabeth Clay, one of ye orphans, which were given her by her grandfather.

Horses &c set apart by Charles Clay for ye children in lieu of two mares with increase, given them by their grand father, John Wilson Sen. dec'd.

By the following extract from the will of Hannah Clay, the statement made by General Green Clay concerning the age of her son Henry is verified :

I give to John Clay, Thomas Clay, Henry Clay and Charles Clay, my sonns, each of them, one cow of four years old, with calf, or calf by her side, to be paid at *attainment of age*, and to John, Thomas and Henry, each of them, one well-fixed gun, and at ye same time and to my daughter, Judith, six new three-pound pewter dishes, at her marriage or Time of age.

The two daughters, Mary and Elizabeth, were probably the only children of age.

The Marke appointed to John Clay, by his Mother, is "a flower de luce, on ye left ear of his hogs or cattle, and a crop and a hole on ye right ear." And liberty is, by his said Mother, requested that ye same may be entered on record. (Henrico County, Xber I. 1687, page 472.)

Charles and Hannah (Wilson) Clay had issue :

      I. MARY CLAY.
      II. ELIZABETH CLAY.
      III. JOHN CLAY; lived on lower side of Deep Creek, Amelia County.
3.   IV. THOMAS CLAY, Test. 1726, of Prince George County (now Amelia, cut off 1734).
4.   V. HENRY CLAY, Test. 1764, in Cumberland County, Virginia.
5.   VI. CHARLES CLAY, Test. 1754, Chesterfield County, Virginia.
      VII. JUDITH CLAY.

3. Thomas Clay had grants of land, July 15, 1717, and June 2, 1722, on upper side of Namozine Creek, which he willed to his son James. Thomas Clay's will was recorded in Prince George County (now Amelia), November 8, 1726, and bore date June 6, 1726. The records of Amelia County are filled with the names of his descendants and those of his brother Charles. His legatees were his children :

6.   I. CHARLES CLAY, of Amelia, and Mary, his wife, deeded to William Cousins, on December 29, 1756, land "inherited from my brother James."
      II. JAMES CLAY ; died before December, 1756, unmarried.
7.   III. JOHN CLAY. His will was recorded in Amelia, October 12, 1782.
      IV. DOROTHY CLAY.
      V. PHŒBE CLAY.
      VI. HANNAH CLAY.

Left "my brother Henry sole executor."

4. Henry Clay was born about 1672, and died at "The Raells," August 3, 1760, of "the nattles," aged eighty - eight years. He was married about 1708 – 9 to Mary Mitchell, daughter of William and Elizabeth Mitchell, who lived and died and were buried in Chesterfield County, on the west side of Swift Creek, on the farm afterward occupied by Reverend Eleazer Clay. Mary Mitchell was born January, 1693, and died "of flux," August 7, 1777. (General Green Clay's Manuscript.)

Henry Clay's will was signed March 28, 1749, and probated at the September term of Chesterfield Court, 1760. The following extracts from it may be interesting :

I, Henry Clay, of Henrico County, being of perfect health, mind, and memory, thanks be to God therefor, and calling to mind my mortality, and knowing that it is appointed unto all men once to die, do make and ordain this my last will and testament, that is to say, *princably* and first of all I give my soul into the hands of God that gave it, and as for my body I commend it to the earth, to be buried in a Christian - like and decent form at the discretion of my executors, nothing doubting but at the general Resurrection I shall receive the same again by mighty power of God ; and as touching my worldly goods wherewith it has pleased God to bless me in this life, I give, devise, and dispose of the same in manner and form following :

Primis. I give and bequeath unto my son, William Clay, the land and plantation whereon he now lives, and my land and plantation on Deep Creek, in Henrico County, whereon Richard Belcher now lives, to him, his heirs, and assigns forever.

Item. I give and bequeath to my son, Henry Clay, the land and plantation he now lives on, and two hundred acres of land at Letalone, in Goochland County, it being the Lower Survey belonging to me at the said Letalone, to him, his heirs and assigns forever.

Item. I give and bequeath unto my son, Charles Clay, the plantation whereon he now lives and all of the land on the north side of Swift Creek and the lower side of Nuttree Run to me belonging, and also four hundred acres at Letalone, it being my Upper Survey at Letalone, to him and his heirs forever.

Item. I give and bequeath unto my son, John Clay, the plantation whereon he now lives and all my land on the north side of Swift Creek and upper side of Nuttree Run, to him and his heirs forever.

Item. I likewise give and bequeath my Grist Mill on Nuttree Run to be equally divided between my son Charles and my son John Clay, to be held in joint tenancy, to them and their heirs forever.

Item. I give to my daughter, Amey Williamson, five pounds, current money.

Item. I give to my daughter, Mary Watkins, five pounds, current money.

Item. I give to my grandson, Henry Clay (Dr. Henry Clay, of Ky.), 240 acres adjoining the lands of James Hill &c.

Item. I give and bequeath to my granddaughter, Mary Clay, daughter of Charles Clay (afterwards Mrs. Stephen Lockett), one negro girl, named Phœbe.

Item. I give unto Mary, my well-beloved wife, the plantation whereon I now live, during her natural life, and my negroes, Lewis, Jo, Sue, Nann, Jenny and Sarah, during her natural life, and what stock and household goods she pleases to have or make use of, of mine.

Item. I devise that the rest of my slaves not heretofore given, and my stock and household goods, be given and equally divided among my four sons aforementioned, at their discretion, and also the negroes above written, and gave my wife, may be equally divided after my wife's decease.

Item. I give to my four sons, above written, and to my wife, to be equally divided, all the ready money and money out at use, that I shall be possessed with at my death.

Item. After my wife's decease I give my plantation, whereon I now live, to my son John Clay and his heirs forever, together with the adjacent lands thereunto belonging, and I do hereby make, constitute and ordain my four sons, above written, to be my only and sole executors of this, my last Will and Testament.

The sons were granted letters of administration on the oaths of George Farrar and Allyson Clarke, witnesses. B. Watkins was Clerk of Chesterfield County at that time.

Henry Clay, of this will, is the common ancestor of the Clays of Kentucky, being the grandfather of Doctor Henry Clay, of Bourbon, of Honorable Henry Clay,* of Ashland, of General Green Clay, of Madison, and of Captain Thomas Clay, of Daviess County, Kentucky.

Doctor Henry and General Green Clay were also first cousins, through their mothers, Lucy and Martha Green, who were sisters, and the daughters of Thomas and Elizabeth (Marston) Green, of Amelia County, Virginia. (See Elizabeth Green's will, probated January, 1760, in Amelia.)

* Great-grandson.

Henry and Mary (Mitchell) Clay had issue, named here according to the will :

       I. WILLIAM MITCHELL CLAY.
8. II. HENRY CLAY, of Southam Parish, Cumberland. (Test. 1764.)
9. III. CHARLES CLAY, died in Powhatan February 25, 1789.
10. IV. JOHN CLAY, of Dale Parish, Chesterfield. (Test. 1761.)
       V. AMEY CLAY, married ——— Williamson.
       VI. MARY CLAY, married ——— Watkins.

5. Charles Clay, senior, of Dale Parish, Chesterfield, son of Charles and Hannah (Wilson) Clay, signed his will January 28, 1754, which was recorded in Chesterfield, August, 1765. He gives his homestead to his beloved wife, Sarah. Mary Clay, the daughter of his son, Henry Clay, deceased, is to receive her father's part. Issue :

       I. THOMAS CLAY, to whom his father deeded, May 5, 1752, two hundred and fifty acres of land in Amelia County.
       II. CHARLES CLAY, to whom his father deeded, May 5, 1752, two hundred and fifty-two acres of land in Amelia.
       III. WILLIAM CLAY, to whom his father deeded, May 5, 1752, two hundred and fifty-two acres of land in Amelia.
11. IV. JAMES CLAY inherited the homestead at his mother's death. He died in 1790. (Ancestor of Governor Clay, of Alabama.)
       V. JUDITH CLAY received fifty acres adjoining her brother, Thomas.
       VI. HENRY CLAY, Vestryman of Dale Parish, Chesterfield County, 1751.

William Clay and Ann, his wife, make deed, September 6, 1764, to a part of these lands, inherited from his father.

June 26, 1765, William Clay makes deed to his son, Obed, of lands on Deep Creek, without his wife's signature.

May 2, 1771, William Clay, of Bedford, made deed to Eleazer Clay; Mary Clay, probably daughter of Henry, was witness. William must have moved later to Franklin County, where we find his will recorded October 5, 1810, in which he mentions wife, Milly (probably second wife), and eight children, viz: Patsy Woodall, Betty Hodges, Hannah Tyree, Judith Clay, Milly Cowden, William Clay, John Clay, heirs of son, Matthew Clay, deceased, and Ezekiel Clay. John Clay, seventh child, married and had Lemuel Clay (who died in 1871, leaving issue), and Sally Clay, who married —— Mitchell. Ezekiel Clay, ninth child, had William B. Clay (who died in 1862, leaving Lizzie and Nathaniel Clay), and Mary Clay, who married —— Wigginton.

6. Charles Clay, of Amelia (son of Thomas, of Charles and Hannah), and Mary, his wife, made deed to William Cousins to two tracts of land which were granted to his father, Thomas Clay, July 15, 1717, and June 2, 1722, on the upper side of Nannersend Creek. "These tracts were willed by the said Thomas Clay, now deceased, to his son, James, my brother, who died without issue." (Deed recorded December 29, 1756.)

January 18, 1791, deeds were recorded in Amelia, showing that the children of Charles Clay, senior, of Amelia, were :

  I. PETER CLAY, of Chesterfield.
  II. DANIEL CLAY, of Lunenburg, whose descendants live in Bedford County.
  III. JESSE CLAY, of Amelia, who died in 1819, leaving issue : Edward, William, John, Daniel, Anderson, Mrs. Henry Jones Wells, Mrs. Frances Archer, and Mrs. Dolly Coleman.
  IV. CHARLES CLAY, JUNIOR, of Amelia.
  V. ELIZA WORSHAM.
  VI. HANNAH AVERY.
  VII. PATTY SNEAD.
  VIII. ANNE CLAY, who married a Clay.

---

7. John Clay, whose will was probated in Amelia County, October 12, 1782. His legatees were his wife, Sarah, the daughter of James Chappell, to whom he left two hundred and fifty acres of land on Deep Creek. Issue :

  I. JOHN CLAY, JUNIOR.
  II. AMEY CLAY CLEMENT.
  III. SARAH CLAY.
  IV. MARTHA CLAY.
  V. DOROTHY CLAY.
  VI. PHŒBE CLAY, who married Philip Johnson.

---

8. Henry Clay, of Southam Parish, Cumberland County, son of Henry and Mary (Mitchell) Clay, of Chesterfield, signed his will March 8, 1764, which was probated October 22, 1764. He married, in 1735, Lucy Green,

born 1717, daughter of Thomas Green and Elizabeth Marston (born November 25, 1672, died August 11, 1759), daughter of Thomas Marston, Justice of Henrico in 1682, and his wife, Elizabeth Marvell. Thomas Green was born about 1665, and died in 1730; was the son of Thomas Green, "the Sea Gull" (so called from having been born upon the sea en route to America), and his wife, Martha Filmer, daughter of Major Henry Filmer, officer of the British army of occupation. (See General Green Clay's manuscript, written about 1820.) Thomas Green, "the Sea Gull," was the son of Thomas and Martha Green, immigrants from Holland, who settled near Petersburg, Virginia.

Major Henry Filmer and his wife, Elizabeth, married in England. They settled in James City County, which he represented in the House of Burgesses in 1642. (Hening's Statutes.)

Henry Clay mentions as the legatees of his will his wife, Lucy, and their children:

12.   I. HENRY CLAY, born, 1736, moved to Kentucky in 1787, died in 1820.
13.   II. CHARLES CLAY, an early emigrant to Kentucky.
       III. SAMUEL CLAY, member of the North Carolina Legislature, 1789–90.
       IV. THOMAS CLAY, of Cumberland County.
       V. ABIA CLAY, Lieutenant in the Revolutionary Army. (He was called also Obia and Abijah.)

14.   VI. MARSTON CLAY, married Elizabeth Williams, of Halifax County.
      VII. REBECCA CLAY.
    VIII. JOHN CLAY, a Captain in the Revolution in 1777.
      IX. ELIJAH CLAY is mentioned in deeds July 13, 1783, and August 2, 1792, when he sells lands in Cumberland County.
       X. LUCY CLAY.

July 28, 1750, Thomas Green, of Amelia, deeds to Henry Clay, of Cumberland, two hundred acres of said Green's Patent of February 10, 1748.

November 4, 1760, Henry Clay, senior, and Lucy, his wife, deed to Henry Clay, junior (Doctor Henry, of Kentucky), two hundred acres on the north side of the Appomattox, formerly granted "to my father, Henry Clay, deceased, July 9, 1724, whereon my son Henry now lives."

In deeds of November, 1758, and 1760, Lucy, the wife of Henry Clay, and Martha, the wife of Charles Clay, are identified as the daughters of Elizabeth Green, deceased, whose will was probated January 24, 1760, in Amelia County.

9. Charles Clay, son of Henry and Mary (Mitchell) Clay, was born January 31, 1716, and died in Powhatan County, Virginia, February 25, 1789. He married Martha Green, November 11, 1741. She was born November 25, 1719, and died September 6, 1793. She was the sister

of Lucy Green, the wife of Henry Clay. (See 8 for her lineage.) Issue :

15.   I. MARY CLAY, born September 22, 1742; married Stephen Lockett.

16.   II. ELEAZER CLAY (Baptist minister), born August 4, 1744.

17.   III. CHARLES CLAY (Episcopal minister), born December 24, 1745.

    IV. HENRY CLAY, born March 5, 1748; died in Trenton, New Jersey, in 1777, while a soldier of the Revolution.

18.   V. THOMAS CLAY, born July 30, 1750; married Polly Callahan, late Dawson.

    VI. BETTIE CLAY, born April 20, 1752; married Alexander Murray.

    VII. LUCY CLAY, born April 20th (twin of Bettie); married William Thaxton.

19. VIII. MATTHEW CLAY, born March 25, 1754; married (1) Polly Williams, (2) —— Saunders.

20.   IX. GREEN CLAY, born August 14, 1757; married Sally Lewis. (To him the Clay family owes tribute as its first historian.)

    X. PRISCILLA CLAY, born April 30, 1759; died unmarried.

    XI. MARTHA CLAY (called Patsy), born July 13, 1761; died in 1844. Married Hopkins Lewis. No issue.

May 21, 1767, Charles Clay, senior, of Cumberland, deeds to Lucy Clay and Bettie Clay (twin daughters) a negro girl apiece as a gift. Witnesses: Marston Clay and Henry Clay.

October 1, 1765, Charles Clay and Martha, his wife, deed to their son, Eleazer, four hundred and twenty-five acres on north side of Nuttree Run and north side of Swift Creek, "land willed me by my father, Henry Clay."

10. John Clay, of Dale Parish, Chesterfield County, "in perfect mind and memory," made his will November 15, 1761, which was probated November, 1762, and proved by the oaths of Thomas Hall and Francis Lockett, witnesses thereto. He disposed of his property as follows:

Item. After payment of debts &c, I give and bequeath to my son, John Clay, four hundred acres of land lying on the south side of Swift Creek, being the plantation whereon my father formerly lived, and three negroes, Hager, Daniel and Lucy, with their increase.

Item. I Give and bequeath to my son Edward, two hundred acres lying on Dumplin Branch, and three negroes,— Jim, Combo and Agathy, with their increase, &c.

Item. I give and bequeath to Jeremiah Bass, son of Mary Bass, now my wife, two hundred acres of land, on the head of Dumplin Branch adjoining the road, and three negroes, Peter, Chance and Fiby, &c. &c.

Item. I leave to my beloved wife, Mary, the use of this plantation, whereon I now live, and three negroes, Indian Peter, Indian Jude and Phillis, and the whole benefit of the Grist Mill, on Nuttree Run, which is my part, now, during her life or widowhood, and after her decease or marriage, the land and mill to fall to my son Edward Clay, to him and his heirs forever.

Item. All the rest and remainder of my negroes to be equally divided among my four children, John Clay, Edward Clay, Jeremiah Bass and Fanny Clay, and all of my household goods and stock of horses, cattle, hogs and sheep to be equally divided between Mary, my wife (she to have a child's part), and John, Edward, Jeremiah and Fanny.

Item. I desire that my estate shall not be appraised, and appoint Francis Mossley (or Moseley) and my son, John Clay, executors.

He had issue :

21.   I. JOHN CLAY, the father of Henry Clay, the statesman.
22.   II. EDWARD CLAY.
    III. FANNY CLAY.

---

11. James Clay, son of Charles Clay, senior, of Chesterfield County, Virginia, was born in Hanover County, and died in 1790. Married Margaret Muse. Issue :

  I. JEREMIAH CLAY, married and had issue : Betsy Clay, married —— Nunnally, and Sabina Clay, married Zachariah Lea.
  II. JAMES CLAY, married and had issue : Nancy Clay; married David Lea.
  III. PATTIE CLAY.
  IV. WILLIAM CLAY, born in Chesterfield, August 11, 1760; married Rebecca Comer in 1787, and died August 4, 1841. Was a soldier of the Revolution, enlisting at sixteen years of age. He made application for a pension October 10, 1832, at which time he was residing in Granger County, Tennessee, and was seventy-two years old. His pension was allowed for seven months' actual service as a private, and one month's service as a Sergeant in the Virginia troops, Revolutionary War. Part of the time he served under Captain Edward Mosely and Colonel Robert Goode. He enlisted in Chesterfield County, Virginia. (Bureau of Pensions, Washington, D. C.) Issue :
    I. MARGARET CLAY.
    II. NANCY CLAY.
    III. MICAJAH CLAY.
23.   IV. CLEMENT COMER CLAY, born 1789.
    V. SAMUEL CLAY.
    VI. ANDERSON CLAY.
24.   VII. CYNTHIA CLAY, born December 15, 1803; died November 21, 1873.

12. Henry Clay, M. D., was born in Cumberland County, Virginia, in 1736, and died in Bourbon County, Kentucky, January 17, 1820, aged eighty-four years. Married in Virginia, in 1754, Rachel Povall, who died April 27, 1820, aged eighty-one years. He moved to Charlotte County, Virginia, between September 26, 1769, and February 15, 1771 ; came to Kentucky in 1787, and located in Clintonville Precinct, Bourbon County, then in a state of nature, densely covered with cane. He is remembered as a tall man with broad shoulders and commanding mein, clad "in doublet and hose, knee breeches and buckles," which style of dress he wore until his death in 1820. For the first year after their arrival he and his family lived in a stockade. The old stone house built and occupied by him is yet standing and in use upon the farm still in the possession of his descendants. Near by is the old family burying-ground, a lot of one acre, enclosed by a substantial stone wall. In it the old pioneers and many of their descendants sleep, awaiting the Resurrection. By the will of his grandson, Henry Clay, a fund is set apart for its repair and preservation, and in the division of his lands that acre is purposely omitted, therefore will remain a graveyard.

Rachel Povall had two brothers, one of whom figured in Virginia history as a man of accomplishments, member

Mrs. LUCRETIA HART CLAY   Honorable THOMAS HART CLAY.

of Congress, etc. He must have been a favorite, for many of the descendants of Doctor Clay still bear his name — Francis Povall. The following incident bespeaks his courage and nobility : He was opposed to dueling, but, being challenged, accepted and met his antagonist upon the field. At the signal the latter fired, missing Povall, who deliberately discharged his weapon in the air, saying he could not take the life of his fellow-man. He died in New Orleans, and with his death the male line became extinct.

Doctor Clay's will, signed August 7, 1809, and probated at the February Court, 1820, is on record in Bourbon County. He mentions his wife, Rachel, and their issue :

25.   I. ELIZABETH CLAY, born January 13, 1755 ; married John Bruce.
26.   II. JOHN CLAY, born February 29, 1757 ; married Patsy Ingram.
27.   III. REBEKAH CLAY, born March 17, 1759 ; married William Finch.
28.   IV. SAMUEL CLAY, born May 10, 1761 ; married Nancy Winn.
         V. RACHEL CLAY, born June 19, 1763 ; married Barkley Martin. No issue.
29.   VI. SALLY CLAY, born November 16, 1765 ; married Matthew Martin.
30.   VII. TABITHA CLAY, born November 15, 1767 ; married Benjamin Bedford.
31.   VIII. MARY ANN CLAY, born March 10, 1770 ; married Thomas Dawson.
32.   IX. HENRIETTA CLAY, born February 2, 1771 ; married George M. Bedinger.
33.   X. MATTIE CLAY, born September 8, 1772 ; married Littleberry Bedford.
34.   XI. HENRY CLAY, JUNIOR, born September 14, 1779 ; married Peggy Helm.
35.   XII. LETTY CLAY, born October 5, 1782 ; married Archibald Bedford.

12

13. Charles Clay emigrated to Fayette County, Kentucky, at an early day. He married —— Lewis, probably a sister of Hopkins Lewis, who married Patsy Clay, the daughter of Charles and Martha Green Clay, of Powhatan County, Virginia, and the sister of General Green Clay. In returning to Virginia on business he was murdered, leaving a wife and several children. Of these:

           I. CLARISSA CLAY, married Elisha Stewart.
36.   II. TEMPERANCE CLAY.

14. Marston Clay married Elizabeth, daughter of John Williams, of Halifax County, Virginia, March 29, 1771. The name is signed "Maston" in the marriage bond. Issue:

37.   I. DIANA COLEMAN CLAY.

15. Mary Clay, born September 22, 1742; died September 5, 1823. Married November 2, 1760, Stephen Lockett (born November 14, 1733; died September 14, 1794), son of Thomas (died 1774) and Elizabeth (Townes) Lockett, and grandson of Thomas and Martha (Osborne) Lockett. Issue:

38.   I. OSBORNE LOCKETT, born May 20, 1769.
39.   II. EDMOND LOCKETT, born August, 1771.
           III. LUCY LOCKETT, born September 8, 1773; married Colonel John Bibb, February 25, 1790.

IV. Henry Wilson Lockett, M. D., born February 19, 1775; married (1) Susan Watkins, and had Betsy Lockett (married F. Smith) and Napoleon Lockett (married Mary, daughter of Colonel Samuel Lockett).

V. Martha Lockett, born July 7, 1780; married Thomas Morton.

VI. Colonel Samuel Lockett, born July 30, 1782; married Selina A. Watkins, and had

    I. Mary Lockett; married Napoleon Lockett.

    II. Frances Lockett; married W. A. Jones, and had Selina Jones and a son.

    III. A daughter; married C. F. Johnson.

    IV. Selina Lockett; married G. W. Roberts.

---

16. Reverend Eleazer Clay, born August 4, 1744; married (1) Jane Apperson; (2) Elizabeth Whitehead, widow of the late E. Swepton (or Swepson); (3) late in life (February 13, 1826), Phœbe Newby, who survived him a few years. He died May 2, 1836; was a distinguished Baptist minister and a man of wealth. His tomb bears record of the fact that he was a soldier in the French and Indian Wars, and fought valiantly throughout the Revolution. His will was probated May 5, 1838, in Chesterfield. He had ten children by his first wife. Issue known:

40.   I. Phineas Clay.

    II. Colonel Samuel Clay, long a Justice of Chesterfield; died January 21, 1831, aged fifty-two years. He married March 3, 1802, Martha Burfoot, daughter of Thomas Burfoot.

III. MATTHEW CLAY; married Miss Turpin, sister of Phineas' wife. Issue :

    I. HARRIET CLAY; married Alfred Mann. Issue : Alfred Mann, junior.

    II. LOUISE CLAY; married William Johnson. Issue : Apperson, Wilbert, and Bettie Johnson.

    III. MATTHEW CLAY, a prisoner of war at Camp Chase during Civil War.

    IV. DOCTOR —— CLAY.

IV. LAVINIA CLAY; married Robert Aikin. Issue : Eleazer, William, Robert, Edward T., and Mary Aikin.

41.   V. JANE CLAY; married October 2, 1797, Edward Trabue.

VI. DORCAS CLAY; married —— Graves, and left issue.

VII. CYNTHIA CLAY; married Daniel Sullivan, of Danville, Virginia. Their daughter married Robert Moon, of Albemarle ; issue, a daughter, who married James Clarke, of Ohio ; issue, Reverend Frank Pinkey Clarke, Rector of an Episcopal Church in Philadelphia.

42. VIII. ANN CLAY; married John C. Russell, and died November 3, 1817.

    [Reverend Eleazer Clay had by his marriage with Mrs. Swepton:]

IX. MARTHA SWEPTON CLAY, born March 30, 1789 ; died, 1824 ; married December 4, 1803, Lawson Burford. Issue :

    I. ELEAZER T. BURFORD, born June, 1805.

    II. ELIZA MATILDA BURFORD, born January 25, 1807.

    III. ELIZABETH FRANCES BURFORD, born October 25, 1808.

    IV. LAWSON McK. BURFORD, died June, 1813.

    V. MARY A. M. BURFORD, born January 6, 1814.

    VI. LAWSON M. BURFORD, born March 14, 1816.

    VII. SUSAN G. BURFORD, born September 25, 1819.

    VIII. OCTAVIA J. BURFORD, born May 6, 1822.

    IX. JOHN BURFORD, JUNIOR, born July 16, 1824 ; died September 24, 1824.

17. Charles Clay, born December 24, 1745; married Editha Davies (born April, 1777), daughter of Henry

Landon and Anne Clayton Davies (married January 15, 1767). Henry Landon Davies was son of Nicholas and Catherine Whiting Davies. His wife, Anne Clayton, was a daughter of John Clayton, the botanist (and his wife, Elizabeth Whiting), son of John Clayton, for many years Attorney - General of Virginia. Charles Clay was an Episcopal minister, ordained by the Bishop of London in 1769; rector of St. Anne's Parish, Albemarle County, from October 22, 1769, to 1784. An earnest patriot, he declared that the "cause of liberty was the cause of God." He created much enthusiasm in behalf of American independence by preaching from the text, "Cursed be he who keepeth back his sword from blood in this war." His will, signed November 12, 1819, probated March 27, 1819, in Bedford, mentions "my small silver can, presented me by my Honorable Friend, Thomas Jefferson, late President of the United States," which he leaves to his son Paul. He makes no provision for a tomb or monument, as stated by Bishop Meade; appoints wife, Editha, and sons, Junius A. and Odin G. Clay, executors. Witnesses were Charles G. Cobbs, John North, Hector Harris, and others. He died in Bedford in 1820. Issue:

        I. JUNIUS AXEL CLAY.
43.   II. ODIN GREEN CLAY.

III. PAUL A. CLAY; was minister of Manchester Parish, Chesterfield County; had sons and daughters. Of them, Paulus
Aurelius Clay died in 1880. Issue: Editha, Harriet,
Alice, and William Clay, and perhaps others. Editha
married (1) —— Thornton, (2) —— Pugh, and has issue.

IV. CYRUS B. CLAY.

18. Thomas Clay, born July, 1750, was a soldier of
the Revolution. Military land warrant, Number 2278,
bearing date January 23, 1784, was issued to him for
three years' service as Captain in the Virginia State Line.
It called for four thousand acres of land. He and his
brother, General Green Clay, were both members of the
First Constitutional Convention of Kentucky. He married Polly Callahan, late Polly Dawson. Issue:

44.   I. NESTOR CLAY, of Texas.
45.   II. TACITUS CLAY, of Texas.
46.   III. CYNTHIA CLAY; married Robert McCreery, of Daviess County.

19. Matthew Clay, son of Charles and Martha (Green)
Clay, was born March 25, 1754; married (1) Polly Williams, (2) —— Saunders; was a devoted patriot and served
throughout the Revolution; was Ensign in the Ninth Virginia October 1, 1776; Second Lieutenant First Virginia
Regulars March 16, 1778; Regimental Quartermaster December, 1778; was retired January, 1783; represented his
district in Congress, and died in Halifax County in 1815.
His daughter lost her life in the burning of the Richmond
Theater December 26, 1811. Other issue unknown.

20. General Green Clay was born August 14, 1757; died October 21, 1828; married March 14, 1795, Sally Lewis (born, 1776; died, 1867), daughter of Thomas Lewis (born March 8, 1749), who married Elizabeth Payne October 27, 1773. Thomas Lewis died in 1809, and his wife March 24, 1827. (See sketch of Douglas Payne Lewis.) Green Clay was the first Deputy Surveyor of Kentucky. In 1788 he was sent as a delegate from Madison County to the Virginia Convention, which ratified the Constitution of the United States. He was a man of great energy, and as a legislator endeavored to augment the prosperity of the Commonwealth by increasing the means and institutions of learning, by promoting a rapid organization of the militia, and advocating an equal and impartial administration of the law, and particularly of the criminal jurisprudence of the State. He was for twenty years a legislator of Virginia and Kentucky; was Speaker of the Senate of Kentucky in 1807. He accumulated a large estate. He was a soldier in the Revolutionary War, and commanded the Kentucky Militia, consisting of four regiments, under Colonels Boswell, Dudley, Cox, and Caldwell, when sent to reinforce General Harrison in the Northwest during the campaign of 1813, in our second war with Great Britain. The heroism and bravery displayed by General Clay in the attack on Fort

Meigs were worthy of better results than fell to the lot of the American arms on that disastrous day, May 5, 1813, when a thousand men were mercilessly sacrificed to the impetuosity and indiscretion of Colonel Dudley. General Clay had issue:

47.　I. ELIZABETH LEWIS CLAY; married Colonel John Speed Smith.
48.　II. PAULINA CLAY; married William Rodes.
　　III. SALLY ANN CLAY; married (1) Colonel E. Irvine, (2) Honorable Madison C. Johnson. No issue.
49.　IV. SIDNEY PAYNE CLAY.
50.　V. BRUTUS JUNIUS CLAY.
51.　VI. CASSIUS MARCELLUS CLAY.
　　VII. SOPHIA CLAY; died in infancy.

21. John Clay married Elizabeth Hudson about 1765. She was the daughter of George and Elizabeth (Jennings) Hudson, of Hanover County, Virginia. George Hudson's will was dated November 30, 1770, and probated April 14, 1773. Elizabeth Hudson died in May or June, 1781. They had but two children: Mary Hudson, wife of John Watkins, and Elizabeth Hudson, wife of John Clay. After John Clay's death, Elizabeth (Hudson) Clay married Captain Henry, the brother of John Watkins. John Clay's will bears date November 4, 1780, and was probated February 7, 1782. September 29, 1784, Elizabeth Clay appears in court as the wife of Henry Watkins. The following notice of her death

appeared in "The Western Citizen," published at Paris,
Kentucky, in December, 1829:

"Died, in Woodford County, on the 4th instant, Mrs. Elizabeth Watkins, widow of Henry Watkins, her second husband, in
the eightieth year of her age. He preceded her in the termi-
nation of this mortal career only ten days. Few women have
fulfilled better the duties incident to all the relations here below
in which she stood. Few have performed more devotedly, or
for a longer period, those higher duties which, it is to be hoped,
have now obtained their reward above. She was the mother of
Henry Clay."

This is a simple tribute, yet rich in historic significance.
We read between the lines of a long and busy life full
to the brim with love and self-denial, and only sustained
by a strong, enduring faith.

She was married when scarce fifteen years of age, and
left a widow at thirty-two, having borne her husband
nine children. She lived to see her son loved and honored by his State, and a candidate for the highest position
within the gift of the nation, yet in a mother's heart is
born the wish that her days might have been lengthened
until the 22d of June, 1847, when, in that little parlor at
Ashland, amidst a circle of the loved and loving, he
bowed his aged head and received the sacrament of bap-
tism at the hands of the parish priest.

Reverend John Clay, though scarcely more than forty
years of age at the time of his death, was a prominent

13

minister of the Baptist Church. Six of his children,
namely, Betsy Hudson, Henry, George Hudson, Sally,
Molly, and a child born after November 4, 1780, died in
infancy or childhood. Those attaining manhood were:

> 52.   VI. John Clay, of New Orleans; born about 1775.
> 53.   VII. Henry Clay, born April 12, 1777; died June 29, 1852.
>   VIII. Porter Clay, born in 1779, and died at Camden, Arkansas,
>   February 16, 1850. He married (1) Sophia Grosch,
>   who died September 28, 1829, leaving one daughter,
>   Mrs. Taylor, whose descendant, Clay Taylor, lives in
>   Missouri; (2) Mrs. Hardin, who left no issue. Mr. Clay
>   was Auditor of Kentucky in 1822. Later he became a
>   minister of the Baptist Church, to which he devoted his
>   talents and energy during the rest of life.

---

22. Edward Clay, brother of Reverend John Clay,
married Magdalene Trabue, daughter of John James and
Olymphia (Dupuy) Trabue. Issue: John, Samuel, Martha,
James, Francis, Judith, Mary, Phœbe, Edward, and Sarah.
This family moved to Alabama, though some of his
descendants now live in Charlotte County, Virginia.

November 2, 1770, Edward Clay, of Charlotte County,
deeded to Eleazer Clay, of Chesterfield, land on Nuttree
Branch, where John Clay's grist mill once stood.

---

23. Clement Comer Clay was born in Halifax County,
Virginia, in 1789, and moved to Alabama in 1812, where
he became Judge of the Circuit Court, Chief Justice of

the Supreme Court, Speaker of the House of the Legislature, member of the first Constitutional Convention, Governor of Alabama, and United States Senator and Commissioner to write the digest of the State law. He was a man of fine talents and great nobility of character, and is held in loving remembrance and esteem by the people of Alabama. He married, in 1815, Susanna Claiborne Withers, daughter of John Withers, of Kingston, Dinwiddie County, Virginia. John Withers married Mary Herbert Jones, daughter of Frederick Jones and Susanna Harrison (born November 29, 1751). Susanna Harrison was the daughter of General Charles Harrison (who served in the Revolution as a Colonel of Artillery in the Continental Line) and Mary Claiborne (born, 1744), daughter of Colonel Augustine Claiborne and Mary Buller Herbert. (Virginia Historical Magazine, Volume I, page 320.)

Judge Comer and Susanna (Withers) Clay had issue:

54. I. CLEMENT CLAIBORNE CLAY.
55. II. JOHN WITHERS CLAY.
     III. HUGH LAWSON CLAY. No issue.

---

24. Cynthia Clay, born December 15, 1803, married (1) William Barrett; issue: Elizabeth Barrett, who died in childhood; (2) on August 26, 1826, Alston Hunter

Green, who was born March 31, 1789, and died June 22, 1847. Issue:

56.   I. MARY SLEDGE GREENE, born August 17, 1827.
57.   II. CLEMENT COMER CLAY GREENE, born June 13, 1829; died
           October 26, 1889.
     III. ELVIRA CYNTHIA GREENE, born September 17, 1832; died
           February 9, 1837.
58.   IV. WILLIAM AUGUSTINE GREENE, born March 1, 1835; died
           September 27, 1856.
59.   V. CORDELIA ELIZABETH GREENE, born November 10, 1840.

----

25. Elizabeth Clay, born January 13, 1755; married John Bruce (born in Pittsylvania County, Virginia, in 1748) about 1770, in Cumberland County. They were early emigrants to Garrard County, Kentucky, and. tradition says, had sixteen children. Of these:

      I. HENRY CLAY BRUCE; married Polly Clay, of Bourbon County,
          September, 1806. No issue.
     II. JOHN BRUCE; married (1) —— Doty, of Garrard County.
          Issue: Mahala, Thomas, Theresa, and Aristides; mar-
          ried (2) Isabella Boyle. Issue: Ann, Patrick, Henry
          Clay, Isabella, Margaret, Jane, Andrew Jackson, Alex-
          ander, Simon Bolivar, and Robert Bruce.
    III. RICHARD BRUCE; married and moved to Illinois. His second
          wife was Sally Coffin, of Lewis County. Issue: Horatio
          and Robert Bruce.
     IV. HORATIO BRUCE; married (1) Eliza Beasly, in Adams County,
          Ohio. Issue: Horatio, Henry Clay, and Richard; mar-
          ried (2) Elizabeth Collier, of Garrard County. Issue:
          Mary, William, Elizabeth, and Eliza Bruce.
60.   V. ALEXANDER BRUCE; married Amanda Bragg.
     VI. PERRY BRUCE.

VII. GEORGE WASHINGTON BRUCE ; married Mrs. Garland (Nancy Buster), of Virginia. Issue : Thomas Henry Clay, Peregrine Pickle, Horatio, and George Washington Bruce.

VIII. CONSTANTINE BRUCE ; married Sophia Williams, of Garrard County, and died without issue.

IX. TABITHA BRUCE ; married —— Arnold. Issue : John, Thomas, and Brunette Arnold.

X. MAHALA BRUCE ; married —— Jamison.

XI. BRUNETTE BRUCE ; married Benjamin Proctor and died without issue.

XII. REBECCA BRUCE ; married Burton Palmer, and had Nixon, John, Patsy, and perhaps others.

XIII. —— BRUCE ; married —— King, and had John and Adriel King.

26. John Clay, born February 29, 1757 ; married Patsy Ingram, and lived and died about a mile from Thatcher's Mill, in Bourbon County. Of his children we know :

I. JOHN CLAY, who moved to Missouri in 1835; married Patsy Eldridge, December 3, 1821.

II. SAMUEL CLAY ; married Rachel Finch, September 4, 1817, and moved to Tennessee. They had Martha, Mary, Nancy, Rachel, Povall, Rebecca, Samuel, and Henry Clay. Rebecca married Thomas Bedford.

III. GEORGE W. CLAY ; married in Fayette County, Kentucky, October 25, 1820, Rebecca Winn, daughter of George and Mildred Winn, and granddaughter of George and Lettice Winn, of Fayette County, Kentucky. The will of George Winn, senior, signed February 20, 1801, and probated at the August Court, 1805, is a very peculiar instrument from the present standpoint, inasmuch as his large estate is willed entirely to his sons and sons-in-law, Thomas Winn, Henry Cotton, John Hancock, Samuel Clay, Jehoidah Musick, Edward Bradley, William Herndon, John Hendley, and George and Adam Winn. His daughters are not mentioned. George W. and Rebecca (Winn) Clay had issue:

    I. THOMAS H. CLAY; married (1) Miss Carpenter, (2) Miss Winn, (3) Miss Fry.

61.   II. JAMES MITCHELL CLAY, born in 1824, of Plattsburg, Missouri.

    III. ELIZABETH CLAY; married William Davenport.

    IV. MILDRED CLAY; married Ratliffe Fisher.

    V. GEORGIA A. CLAY; married Marion Hundley.

---

27. Rebecca Clay, born in 1759; married William Finch. Issue:

62.   I. NANCY FINCH; married Zephaniah Robnett in 1810.

    II. REBECCA FINCH; married E. Offutt. No issue.

    III. RACHEL FINCH; married Samuel Clay, of Tennessee.

63.   IV. HENRY FINCH; married Cynthia Collier.

    V. JOHN FINCH, a soldier in the War of 1812 in Captain Garrard's Company.

    VI. JAMES FINCH (twin with John), also a soldier in the War of 1812.

    VII. THOMAS FINCH; moved to Tennessee and left issue.

    VIII. WILLIAM FINCH; moved to Tennessee and left issue.

    IX. ZACHARIAH FINCH, of Bourbon County; married Elizabeth Scott.

    X. ADAM FINCH, of Bourbon County, was three times married: (1) Mrs. Bedford, nee Throgmorton, of Nicholas County.

---

28. Samuel Clay, born May 10, 1761, came to Kentucky soon after the close of the Revolutionary War and settled on Green Creek, Bourbon County. In 1777, when less than sixteen, he enlisted in the Revolutionary Army and followed General Greene throughout the campaign of the Carolinas. He was wounded in the foot at Fort

Watson, and was carried to the home of Mrs. Abram
Martin, in Edgefield District, South Carolina, to be nursed
by his sisters. The Tories, learning of his refuge, searched
the house in vain to find the wounded rebel, and in their
chagrin cut open the feather beds and scattered the contents. His wound healing rapidly, young Clay soon
rejoined his command at Fort Motte, and remembered
the heroine of that victory as she hastened to General
Marion with the bows and arrows for the destruction of
her own home. Many interesting stories have been handed
down respecting his enlistment and service, which were
more than twice-told tales in the home of the writer a
quarter of a century ago.

None of Samuel Clay's descendants doubt his Revolutionary record, yet we have not been able to verify the
family traditions. He was a man of fine physique and
great inventive genius, which served him to good purpose
in pioneer times. He was killed by the falling of tim-
bers while superintending the erection of a new barn.
He married Ann (Nancy) Winn, daughter of George and
Lettice Winn, of Fayette County, Kentucky. His will
was probated in the Bourbon Court, June, 1810. Issue:

64.   I. Henry C. Clay; married Mary Grimes.
65.   II. Letitia Clay.
       III. Samuel Clay; died unmarried.
66.   IV. George Clay, of St. Louis, Missouri.

67.   V. LITTLEBERRY BEDFORD CLAY, of Pleasant Hill, Cass County,
            Missouri.
68.   VI. RICHARD P. CLAY.
69. VII. JOHN CLAY, of Georgia.
     VIII. THOMAS CLAY; died in Milledgeville, Georgia, May 16, 1831.
70.   IX. RACHEL CLAY.
71.   X. WILLIAM GREEN CLAY, born January 1, 1810; married October
            6, 1829, Patsy Bedford (born November 26, 1809),
            daughter of Littleberry and Mattie (Clay) Bedford. Mr.
            Clay died April 17, 1855.   Issue:
         I. THOMAS CLAY.
        II. MARIA E. CLAY; married William R. Colcord. Issue:
                Charles, William, Harry, and Maria L. Colcord.
       III. WILLIAM GREEN CLAY; died June 7, 1862, in the
                Southern Army.
        IV. SIDNEY B. CLAY.
         V. MATTIE V. CLAY; married Francis H. Donaldson.
                Issue: Margaretta, Francis, Grace, and Fred
                Donaldson.

29. Sally Clay, born November 16, 1765, married Matthew Martin, brother of Barkley Martin, who married Rachel Clay. They were the sons of Abram and Elizabeth (Marshall) Martin, of Caroline County, Virginia, who settled in Edgefield District, South Carolina. These sisters are named among the heroines of the Revolution. In May, 1781, only two inland posts in Georgia and South Carolina were in the possession of the British, Pickens and Lee were besieging Augusta, while General Greene sat down before Ninety-Six, so called from being situated ninety-six miles from the chief town of the Cherokee Nation. It was an important place, therefore

strongly fortified. Its garrison was of Tories commanded by Colonel John Cruger, a loyalist from New York, who had rendered himself particularly obnoxious because of his cruel persecution of the patriots. General Greene's approaches were skillfully protected by a "Maham Tower," a high structure of logs which commanded the stockade. Mounted upon this battlement, men from behind the breast-works could pour a destructive fire. As a protection against the sharpshooters, the Tory garrison piled sand-bags high upon the parapets, which were surrounded by a deep, wide moat. The siege was pressed for nearly a month. The defenders were reduced to direst extremi-ties for water, which could only be brought in small quantities at night by a few negroes, entirely nude that they might be invisible in the darkness. General Greene hoped to starve them out and thus save his command further suffering.

May 18, 1781, the Martin family received news that a courier, guarded by two British soldiers, had left Charles-ton with important dispatches for the beleaguered fort. These zealous patriots, women though they were, "put their heads together" and determined to secure those papers. Grace (Waring) and Rachel Clay Martin each donned a suit of her husband's clothes, and, providing herself with contraband arms, took a protected position in a turn of the public road where they knew the escort must pass.

It was already late in the evening, and the shadows of the forest lent additional darkness to the hour, when the tramp of the horses' feet were heard in the distance. We can scarce imagine the feelings of those courageous young women as three well-equipped riders appeared in sight. As the couriers approached the hiding-place the disguised women sprang from their covert, presented their pistols, and claimed the dispatches. The soldiers being completely surprised while off their guard, quickly yielded to the demands of the rebels. Having secured the important documents, together with the guns and accoutrements, they paroled their prisoners and wisely disappeared through the bushes.

Having reached the house and displayed their trophies, Sally Clay Martin claimed the privilege of carrying the dispatches to headquarters. Mounting an old blind pony deemed worthless by both armies, she rode through the darkness to the picket station by midnight. She was quickly ushered into General Greene's presence, and placed the dispatches in his hand. These bore the news that General Rawdon, strengthened by three Irish regiments, had left Charleston to reinforce the fort at Ninety-Six. General Greene, who had scarce two thousand men, realized quickly that he must either abandon the siege or make an immediate attack. He decided on the latter, and asked for a hundred volunteers to scale the walls, and with iron hooks pull down the sand-bags from the parapets. That it was a "forlorn hope" was quickly realized by those brave soldiers, and yet a hundred and twenty responded. Two of this number were Samuel Clay and Barkley Martin. At two o'clock in the morning a vigorous charge was made from three points, which was met by a most spirited and determined resistance. General Greene, realizing that if the fort were taken at all it must be done by the sacrifice of the best material of his army, wisely ordered a hasty retreat. When the command reached High Hills to rest and recruit, it was found that only seven of that heroic hundred answered to roll-call.

At the close of the Revolutionary War, Matthew and Barkley Martin moved to the neighborhood of Columbia, Tennessee. Mrs. Barkley Martin was living in 1849, about eighty-six years of age. She had no children. Matthew and Rachel (Clay) Martin raised a large family, who were prominent in that State. One son, Honorable Barkley Martin, was Representative in Congress from Tennessee. His father lived to a great age, dying in October, 1849, seventy-six years from the day he entered the Revolutionary War.

30. Tabitha Clay, daughter of Doctor Henry and Rachel (Povall) Clay; born November 15, 1761; married Benjamin Bedford (born December 23, 1762), son of Colonel Thomas Bedford (Test. March 7, 1785), and his wife, Mary Coleman. Thomas was the son of Stephen Bedford (Test. March 25, 1758), of Southam Parish, Cumberland County, Virginia. Colonel Thomas Bedford was a member of the Committee of Safety of Charlotte County, appointed January 13, 1775. (See Virginia Historical Magazine, October, 1897.) Benjamin and Tabitha Clay Bedford had issue:

72.   I. BENJAMIN F. BEDFORD; married Eleanor G. Buckner.
      II. JACKSON BEDFORD.
    III. STEPHEN BEDFORD.
    IV. ROBERT BEDFORD. (See 32.)
     V. HARRY BEDFORD.
    VI. THOMAS JEFFERSON BEDFORD.
   VII. NANCY BEDFORD (Mrs. Thornton).
  VIII. SIDNEY BEDFORD.
    IX. MARY BEDFORD (Mrs. Clarkson).
     X. SALLY BEDFORD; married Henry Towles, a brave soldier at the siege of Fort Meiggs.

31. Mary Ann Clay, born March 10, 1770; married Thomas Dawson March 14, 1789. Issue:

73.   I. RACHEL DAWSON; married Rezin Hammond Gist.
    II. LUCINDA DAWSON; married Henry Cohen.
   III. REBECCA DAWSON; married William De Graftenried, of Virginia. Issue:

I. Lucinda H. De Graftenried; married Edwin G.
Bedford. (See 82.)
II. Rachel G. De Graftenried; married George W.
Sydnor. Issue: Martin Sydnor, deceased.
IV. Thomas Dawson; married Lou Anne De Graftenried. Issue:
John B. and Henrietta Dawson.
74. V. Henrietta Dawson; married James Prewitt.

———

32. Henrietta Clay, born February 2, 1771; married
Major George Michael Bedinger of Revolutionary fame.
The Bedinger family is of German descent. The immigrant to this country was Adam Bedinger, born and
married in the village of Dorschel, near Strasburg, in
Alsace, and came with his wife and family to America
in 1736. He settled in Pennsylvania, and acquired wealth
in York County, where he died. Henry Bedinger, second
son of Adam, married early and settled near his father.
He married Mary von Schlegel, a German lady of the
family of Augustus and Frederick William von Schlegel,
who were poets, critics, and philosophers. Augustus was
a celebrated poet and an intimate friend of Madame de
Stael. In 1762 Henry Bedinger and family moved to
Mecklenburg, Frederick County, Virginia. Since then the
names of town, county, and State have all been changed,
and are now Shepherdstown, Jefferson County, West Virginia. His remains lie in the old Episcopal churchyard at
Shepherdstown, and his tomb bears this inscription: "The

ashes of Henry Bedinger, who departed this life January 22, 1772, in the forty-second year of his age." He had three sons who were officers in the Revolutionary Army and served to the close of the war. They were Major Henry Bedinger, Major George Michael Bedinger, and Lieutenant Daniel Bedinger. The latter's commission bears date 14th November, 1776, and on the 14th September, 1778, he was transferred to the Seventh Virginia.

He ran away in the summer of 1776 and enlisted in the army at the age of sixteen. At Brandywine he was taken prisoner by the British, and suffered many hardships which brought on severe sickness. Just after his capture he resented some indignity, and a British officer demanded the name of the impudent young rascal. Daniel replied, "I am, sir, a soldier, a Virginian, and a gentleman," a reply indicative of an undaunted spirit and great self-respect. He was a prisoner for nearly a year, and only liberated when the British evacuated Philadelphia, being left behind them, as they believed, in a dying condition.

Major George Michael Bedinger was an early pioneer of Kentucky. Settled in Nicholas, then a part of Bourbon County. In 1779 acted as Adjutant in the unfortunate expedition of Colonel Bowman against the Indian town of Chillicothe. He was a brave and efficient officer at the Battle of the Blue Licks. In 1792 represented his county in the legislature, and in 1802 was elected to Congress, serving two terms. Retired to private life in 1807. Issue:

    I. HENRIETTA BEDINGER; married Henry Clay. Left no issue.

    II. ELIZABETH BEDINGER; married Robert Bedford (son of Benjamin and Tabitha (Clay) Bedford, and grandson of Thomas and Mary (Coleman) Bedford), and left one son, Robert Bedford, who married —— Rogers, of Nicholas County.

    III. DANIEL P. BEDINGER; settled in Bourbon County, and married, January 20, 1826, his own cousin, Letitia, daughter of Colonel Henry Clay, youngest son of Doctor Henry and Rachel Povall Clay, who emigrated from Virginia in 1787. They had two children:

        I. DANIEL BEDINGER; married Pattie Holloway. No issue.

        II. OLIVIA BEDINGER; married, October 9, 1849, Richard H. Lindsay, and had:

            I. ROSA LINDSAY; married, February 26, 1873, W. S. Buckner, son of William and Sallie Woodford Buckner; grandson of Walker and Elizabeth (Walker) Buckner; great-grandson of Thomas and Elizabeth (Hawes) Buckner, who were married May 25, 1780. William and Rosa Buckner had Olivia, William E., and Sallie Woodford Buckner.

            II. ANNE ELIZABETH LINDSAY; married Asa K. Lewis March 15, 1876. Issue: Richard L. and Frank Lewis.

            III. FRANK LINDSAY, of Nicholas County.

33. Mattie Clay, born September 8, 1772; died March 2, 1864. Married Littleberry Bedford, born in Charlotte

County, Virginia, January 1, 1769, and died in Bourbon County, Kentucky, August 7, 1829. Issue:

I. THOMAS BEDFORD, born October 25, 1790; was a soldier in the War of 1812, and killed in service; a member of Captain William Garrard's Company, Major V. Ball's Squadron of the "State Dragoons."

II. HENRY BEDFORD, born October 26, 1792; married Patsy Dawson May 31, 1810.

75. III. ELIZABETH BEDFORD, born December 7, 1794.

IV. WILLIAM BEDFORD, born December 7, 1796.

76. V. LITTLEBERRY BEDFORD, born July 30, 1798.

77. VI. CAPTAIN JOHN BEDFORD, born July 26, 1800.

78. VII. AUGUSTINE VOLNEY BEDFORD, born August 18, 1802.

79. VIII. FRANKLIN P. BEDFORD, born May 14, 1804. (See 87.)

80. IX. BENJAMIN C. BEDFORD, born August 17, 1807.

X. PATSY BEDFORD, born November 26, 1809. (See 71.)

81. XI. ARCHIBALD M. BEDFORD, born February 25, 1812.

82. XII. EDWIN G. BEDFORD, born August 27, 1814.

XIII. GEORGE M. BEDFORD, born August 27, 1817; married Mary A. Bedford November 4, 1840, daughter of Benjamin F. and Eleanor G. Bedford. Mr. Bedford was a successful financier and a generous rebel during the late war. Issue: Mary E., Julia, Maria, George M., junior, and Benjamin F. Bedford. George Bedford died February 23, 1887.

34. Henry Clay, son of Doctor Henry and Rachel (Povall) Clay, came with his parents at eight years of age to Kentucky. He was born September 14, 1779, and died in Bourbon County in 1863, aged eighty-four years. He served during the War of 1812 under General Harrison as a Second Lieutenant; was a man of great energy and fine judgment, and took much interest in the politi-

Governor CLEMENT COMER CLAY   H   H CLEMENT H

cal issues of his day. While not old enough to vote for the adoption of the second Constitution of Kentucky, in 1799, the late Madison C. Johnson, of Lexington, is authority for the statement that he warmly espoused the idea of incorporating in that instrument a plan for the gradual but ultimate abolition of slavery in Kentucky. It was in that cause, and in Bourbon County, that Henry Clay, of Ashland, made his first political speech.

The advocates of emancipation failed in that contest, but their appeals made a deep impression upon the public mind. Colonel Henry Clay was always a staunch emancipationist, and never sought preferment in any way except in furtherance of that cause; was President of an Emancipation Society; a candidate for the legislature on that ticket; was a staunch Union man, and wanted to enlist on that side at the breaking out of the Civil War, in spite of his extreme age.

He married Margaret (Peggy) Helm, daughter of Joseph Helm, of Lincoln County. To them were born twelve children, one dying in infancy. The others were:

83. I. HENRY CLAY, born June 4, 1798.
84. II. JOHN CLAY, born February 13, 1800.
85. III. SALLY CLAY, born 1801; married William T. Buckner.
86. IV. JOSEPH HELM CLAY, born October 22, 1803.
     V. LETITIA CLAY; married Daniel Bedinger. (See Bedinger line.)
87. VI. HENRIETTA CLAY.
88. VII. ELIZABETH CLAY, born July 8, 1812.

89. VIII. SAMUEL CLAY, born April 8, 1815.
90. IX. MARY ANN CLAY.
91. X. FRANCIS POVALL CLAY, born October 26, 1819.
XI. MATTHEW MARTIN CLAY; married, in 1843, Mary, daughter of Judge Asa K. Lewis. She died in 1879 without issue. Captain Clay commanded a company in the Twenty-first Kentucky Infantry, on the Union side, in the Civil War.

35. Letty Clay, born October 5, 1782; married Archibald Bedford, son of Colonel Thomas and Mary (Coleman) Bedford. Issue:

92. I. THOMAS BEDFORD.
93. II. BENJAMIN BEDFORD.
94. III. HILLARY MOSELY BEDFORD.
95. IV. HENRY C. BEDFORD.
96. V. A. COLEMAN BEDFORD.
VI. GREEN CLAY BEDFORD; married Caroline Chinn, of Fayette County. Issue: Mark, John, Richard Higgins, Rachel, and Susan Bedford. Live in Missouri.
VII. PAUL CLAY BEDFORD; married —— Harris. Issue: Asa, Ashby, Harris, and Susan Bedford.
97. VIII. ASA B. BEDFORD.
98. IX. MARY CLAY BEDFORD.
X. NANCY BEDFORD; married (1) Doctor Bryant, (2) Jonathan F. Payne, of Jefferson County. Issue: Mary, Henrietta, Belle, and Doctor Thomas Payne.
XI. PATSY BEDFORD; married Colonel James Ware, of Bourbon County. Issue:
I. THOMPSON WARE; married Alice Edwards.
II. HENRY B. WARE.
III. JAMES WARE.
IV. SALLIE WARE; married Robert Berry, of Woodford.
V. LUCY WARE.
XII. RACHEL BEDFORD; married Colonel S. G. Stewarts, of South Carolina. Issue: Elizabeth, Ada, Archibald, Benton, and James H. Stewarts.
XIII. HENRIETTA BEDFORD; died unmarried.

36. Temperance Clay married (1) Charles Black, of Maryland.   Issue :

  99.   I. CHARLES CLAY BLACK.
  100. II. STEPHEN BLACK.
  101. III. ELIZABETH BLACK.
         IV. NARCISSUS BLACK ; married Mr. McAfferty, of Chilicothe, Ohio.
         V. GEORGE W. BLACK ; died young.

---

37. Diana Coleman Clay married April 7, 1790, in Halifax County, Virginia, Lieutenant Joseph Ligon, junior, son of Captain Joseph and Judith Ligon.   He served with distinction in the Revolutionary War, and was severely wounded at the Battle of Guilford Court - House, North Carolina.   Had been previously married to Lettice Simms, by whom he had three children.   He emigrated to Tennessee, refusing pension or bounty, declaring he fought for liberty alone.   Issue :

         I. MARSTON LIGON ; died unmarried.
         II. ELIZABETH COLEMAN LIGON ; married Colonel Richard Terry.
         III. DIANA COLEMAN LIGON ; married Doctor Josiah W. Fort, in Robertson County, Tennessee, February 14, 1816.   Issue :
                 I. JACOB HILLIARD FORT, born June 13, 1818 ; died September 3, 1818.
                 II. MARIA PATELLO FORT, born July 29, 1819 ; died September 4, 1819.
  102.   III. HARRIET ELIZABETH FORT, born December 23, 1822.
  103.   IV. SUSAN GREEN FORT, born September 3, 1824.
  104.   V. WILLIAM WARDER FORT, born March 18, 1826.
  105.   VI. DOCTOR JOSEPH MARSTON FORT, born January 11, 1828.

VII. JULIA LETTICE FORT, born December 19, 1829; died October 4, 1830.
VIII. JULIA LETTICE MARIA PATELLO FORT, born August 29, 1831; married John R. Rochelle, and had James R. Rochelle, of Texas.
IX. DIANAH COLEMAN FORT, born November 14, 1833; died July 1, 1854.
X. ORRIN DATUS JETHRO BATTLE FORT, born August 18, 1836; died July 26, 1838.

---

38. Osborne Lockett, born May 20, 1769; died in Prince Edward County, Virginia, in 1836. He owned large landed estates and numerous negroes; was several times presiding Magistrate of the county. Judge F. N. Watkins said of him: "He was one of the old people of the county in whom were blended the virtues of a good citizen, and from whom, with his respected brother, Edmund, the 'Lockett Magisterial District' derives its corporate title." He married, February 20, 1801, Agnes Branch Scott, daughter of James Scott and Elizabeth Osborne. The latter was the daughter of William and Elizabeth Tanner Osborne, and the granddaughter of Lodowick Tanner. Issue:

106.		I. FRANCES WILSON LOCKETT, born November 11, 1801; died July 22, 1823.
II. POLLY LOCKETT, born August 20, 1807; married her cousin, Stephen Lockett.
III. MARTHA LOCKETT, born December 20, 1809; married Thomas E. Perkinson. Issue:
I. PATTY PERKINSON; married S. W. Vaughn.
II. MARY PERKINSON; married Joseph Morton. Issue: Ernest and Mary Morton.

IV. ELIZABETH LOCKETT, born December 11, 1811; married P. L. Ligon. Issue: Bettie Ligon and —— Ligon.

V. GEORGE LOCKETT, born December 29, 1815; married Eliza Vaughn. Issue: Fifteen children, all of whom live in Missouri.

VI. LUCY T. LOCKETT, born February 19, 1816; married S. W. Vaughn. Issue:

    I. WILLIAM VAUGHN; married Sallie Blanton, and has issue.

    II. PATTIE VAUGHN; married H. Walton. Issue.

    III. VIRGINIA VAUGHN; married Henry Ligon. Issue.

    IV. MOLLIE VAUGHN; married John Walton. Issue.

VII. AGNES LOCKETT, born February 13, 1818; married T. W. Morton. Issue.

VIII. JAMES LOCKETT, born March 28, 1820; married Mary Clark. Issue:

    I. MARTHA OSBORNE LOCKETT; married Ed. Miller. Issue.

    II. LELIA LOCKETT; married Mr. Monot, of Louisiana. Issue.

    III. JAMES LOCKETT; married, and has issue.

    IV. MARY LOCKETT; married Thomas Garnett. Issue.

IX. BENJAMIN F. LOCKETT, M. D., Demonstrator of Anatomy in Richmond Medical College; died without issue.

X. THOMAS F. LOCKETT; married Sally W. Dixon and lives in Texas, where he has a large family.

---

39. Edmund Lockett (of Stephen and Mary Clay Lockett), born August, 1771, died January 28, 1833; married Elizabeth Walthall. Issue:

    I. NANCY LOCKETT; married Smith Crute.

    II. STEPHEN LOCKETT; married (1) Polly, daughter of Osborne Lockett, (2) Betsy Vaughn.

    III. ELIZABETH LOCKETT; married R. Cunningham.

    IV. CASSANDRA LOCKETT; married N. Crute.

> V. MARY LOCKETT ; married William Wormack.
> VI. MARTHA LOCKETT ; married William Cobbs.
> VII. CHRISTOPHER LOCKETT ; married Josephine Blanton. Issue :
>   Edmund, Harry, and Mary Lockett.
> VIII. EDMUND LOCKETT.

---

40. Phineas Clay married Francis Turpin.   Issue :

> I. JANE CLAY ; married Mr. Walthall.
> II. ELIZABETH CLAY ; married Frank Branch Cheatham. Issue :
>   I. DUNCHIE CHEATHAM ; married —— Holbrook.
>   II. ZACHARIAH CHEATHAM ; married —— Lester.
>   III. SABELIA CHEATHAM ; married —— Atchison, and lives
>   in Woodland, California.
>   IV. JUNIUS CHEATHAM ; married Mrs. Prentice.
>   V. FRANK CHEATHAM ; married —— Wilkinson.
> III. CHARLES CLAY ; married Mary Wilkinson. Issue : Alice,
>   Robert, and Charles (all dead), and Sidney and Hern-
>   don Clay, of Richmond, Virginia.
> IV. JOHN CLAY ; married —— Markham. Issue : Fanny and
>   Artemus Clay.
> V. MARY CLAY ; married William Flournoy. Issue : Clarence,
>   Oscar (dead), and Fanny Flournoy, who married (1)
>   Junius Ellett, (2) —— Smith, and has Ernest Ellett.
> VI. MARTHA CLAY ; married (1) Doctor Hall, (2) Professor W.
>   J. Morrissett, who were the foster-parents of Mary Agnes
>   Clay, of Keachie College, Keachie, Louisiana.
> VII. PHINEAS CLAY ; married Sarah Turpin. Issue : Thomas,
>   Addie, Sallie, Walter, Irving A., and Mary Agnes Clay.
>   The first four died young.

---

41. Jane Clay, daughter of Reverend Eleazer Clay, married Edward Trabue (born 1764), who was a Revolutionary soldier and fought at Guilford Court-House, and was present at Gates' defeat. She died in 1845. Issue :

Edward, Matilda, Susan, Jane, Cynthia (married and had Susan, who married —— Glasscock), Martha, Charles Clay, Doctor John and G. W. Trabue. Of these, Charles Clay Trabue was born in Woodford County, Kentucky, August 27, 1798. In 1818, when volunteers were called for to suppress the Seminole Indians in Florida, he enlisted and followed Jackson during the war. Later he settled in Nashville, and afterward moved to Missouri. Remaining there some years, he again went to Nashville, and became its Mayor in 1839–40. Married, July 5, 1820, Agnes Green Woods. He died November 24, 1851. Issue:

   107.   I. MARTHA A. TRABUE.
   108.   II. ANTHONY E. TRABUE.
          III. JOSEPH W. TRABUE, died unmarried.
   109.   IV. JANE W. TRABUE.
   110.   V. SARAH E. TRABUE.
   111.   VI. CHARLES CLAY TRABUE, JUNIOR.
   112.   VII. ROBERT W. TRABUE.
          VIII. GEORGE W. TRABUE; married Ellen Dunn. Issue:
             I. WILLIAM D. TRABUE; married Lucinda B. O. Bryan. Issue: George O. and William D. Trabue, junior.
             II. GEORGE TRABUE.
             III. CHARLES CLAY TRABUE.
             IV. ANTHONY E. D. TRABUE.

42. Anne Clay, daughter of Reverend Eleazer Clay, married John Coates Russell, son of General William and Tabitha (Adams) Russell, of Culpeper County, Virginia. Anne died November 3, 1817. Mr. Russell died November 17, 1822. Issue:

113.   I. Jane Russell, born July 30, 1794.
114.   II. Tabitha Adams Russell, born June 3, 1796.
        III. Mary C. Russell, born April 12, 1800 ; died young.
115.   IV. Lavinia Green Russell, born April 14, 1803.
116.   V. Doctor William Clay Russell, born December 26, 1806.
        VI. Cynthia A. Russell, born August 13, 1811 ; died July, 1867.

43. General Odin Green Clay (of State Militia) was born about 1795, near the present Forest Depot, Bedford County. From 1827, when he entered the Virginia House of Delegates from Campbell County, his busy, useful, and honored life was constantly before the public eye. He was a member of the House of Delegates for twenty years, and the first President of the old Virginia & Tennessee Railroad. No man ever more thoroughly deserved or more universally received the implicit confidence of the community. He married, October 9, 1822, his first cousin, Anne C. E. Davies (born June 12, 1803, and died October 26, 1848), daughter of Samuel Boyle and Elizabeth (McCulloch) Davies. Samuel Boyle Davies was the grandson of John Clayton (1693–1773), son of John Clayton (1665–1737), Attorney-General of the Colony of Virginia ; son of Sir John Clayton by his wife, Alice, daughter of Sir William Bowyer, of Denham Bucks, Baronet, by his wife, Margaret, daughter of Sir John Weld, of Arnolds, son of Sir Humphrey Weld. These Welds were founders of Virginia. Issue: One daughter and six sons,

four of whom were in the Second Virginia Cavalry, Army of Northern Virginia, 1861–1865 :

> I. CYRUS BEVERLY CLAY; married Mary Coles Meriwether, and had Lizzie, Mary, Nannie, and Boyle Clay, and perhaps others.
> II. DEWITT CLINTON CLAY; married, in 1852, Elizabeth Noble Lee, of Bedford County, Virginia, and died in 1870, leaving issue :
>> I. ODIN GREEN CLAY, born January 25, 1855 ; a lawyer of St. Paul, Minnesota.
>> II. MARY LEE CLAY, born December, 1856.
>> III. ANN CLAYTON CLAY, born June 1, 1858; married James A. Meriwether, of Springfield, Missouri.
>> IV. SALLY MANSON CLAY, born October 11, 1861.
> III. SAMUEL BOYLE CLAY; died, leaving Catherine, Charles Green, and Callie Clay.
> IV. JUNIUS P. CLAY; died unmarried.
> V. CHARLES HENRY CLAY, of Pearch Post-office, Bedford County; married Frances, daughter of John Armstead, of Campbell County, and had Editha (married Samuel Lewis, of Washington, D. C.), Dora, Andrew (lately deceased), DeWitt, Cyrus Douglas, Rufus, Odin, and Charles Clay.
> VI. CALHOUN GREEN CLAY; was killed in the Confederate Army,
> VII. ANN ELIZABETH CLAY; married Frank Thornton, and is now a widow with one son.

44. Nestor Clay, son of Captain Thomas and Polly Callahan Clay, moved to Texas about 1834 and settled in Washington County, and had Tacitus Thomas, Matthew, Mary Jane, and Lucy A. Clay. Tacitus Thomas Clay was a gallant Colonel in the Confederate Army. He married and had issue :

I. Nestor Clay, born June 2, 1855.
II. Samuel Clay; died without issue.
III. Anna Clay.
IV. Mary Robertson Clay, born December 24, 1861; married Decius McCreery March 22, 1892, and has one child, Coralyn Elizabeth McCreery.
V. Carrie Franklin Clay, born February 22, 1865.
VI. Tassie E. Clay, born March 6, 1867; married William G. Thornhill December 2, 1891, and has one child, Tacitus Clay Thornhill, born December 17, 1895.

---

45. Tacitus Clay, son of Captain Thomas and Polly Callahan Clay, married Vibella McCreery, of Kentucky, and had issue:

I. Thomas Clay; married Bettie Robertson, and had Tacitus, Susan A., James, Seth S., Edward F., and Nettie L. Clay.
II. Athius Clay; married Pauline Thornhill, and had Lula L., Alice, Thomas, junior, Kate, Anna Belle, Nestor, and Tacitus Clay, junior.
III. Thetis Clay; married C. Powers, and had Lula Clay and Tula Powers.
IV. Tula Clay; married William Dever, and has twelve children.
V. Lula Clay; married Thomas Haxey, and had Vibella and Thomas Haxey.

---

46. Cynthia Clay married Robert McCreery, and had issue:

117.   I. Thomas Clay McCreery, born 1816; died 1890.
II. Decius McCreery, a soldier of the Mexican War, who died in Arkansas in 1865; married Mary Frances White, of Daviess County, Kentucky, November 11, 1841, and had nine children. She died February 7, 1861, leaving Thomas, Matthew, Decius, Albert, Emma, Malcolm, Green, and Fanny McCreery. Of these:

I. MATTHEW McCREERY; married Virginia Twinage
February 12, 1871, and died June 21, 1898,
leaving Robert, Roger, Roy, and ——.

II. DECIUS McCREERY, born January 7, 1848; married Mary Clay.

III. ALBERT McCREERY; married Maggie Willis, and
has five children.

IV. MALCOLM McCREERY; married Dora Miller, of Lam-
pasas Springs, Texas, and has five children.

47. Elizabeth Lewis Clay married, July 31, 1815, Colonel John Speed Smith, for forty years one of the leading lawyers and prominent men of Eastern Kentucky;
born in Jessamine County, July 3, 1792. He settled in
Richmond when its bar was one of the ablest in the
country, with Martin D. Hardin at its head; was frequently
a member of the Kentucky Legislature, and a Representative in Congress during President Monroe's administration, 1821–23; was appointed by President John Quincy
Adams Secretary of Legation to the United States Minister to the South American Congress assembled at Tacu-
baya; was appointed by President Jackson United States
Attorney for the District of Kentucky; was appointed by
the Kentucky Legislature, January 5, 1839, Joint Commissioner with Ex-Governor Morehead to visit Ohio and
solicit a passage of laws to prevent evil-disposed persons
in that State from enticing away or assisting slaves to
escape from Kentucky, and to provide more efficient

means for recapturing fugitive slaves by their masters or their agents, which mission was eminently successful. In the campaign of 1813 Colonel Smith served as Aide-de-Camp to General Harrison. Issue :

118.   I. SALLY ANN SMITH, born July 10, 1818.
119.   II. CURRAN CASSIUS SMITH, born July 12, 1822.
120.   III. GREEN CLAY SMITH, born July 10, 1827.
121.   IV. PAULINE GREEN SMITH, born September 30, 1829.
      V. JUNIUS BRUTUS SMITH ; died unmarried.
      VI. MARY SPENCER SMITH ; died unmarried.
      VII. JOHN SPEED SMITH.

48. Pauline Green Clay, born September 7, 1802 ; married, November 3, 1819, William Rodes (born February 24, 1794), son of Robert Rodes (born May 11, 1759) and Eliza Delany, his wife (born January 29, 1759), who were married May 30, 1782. Robert Rodes was a Captain of a company from Albemarle County, Virginia, assigned to the defense of the Atlantic Coast during the Revolution. Robert Rodes was the son of John Rodes (born November 6, 1729), who married, September 9, 1754, Sarah Harris, born May 24, 1736. John Rodes was the son of John Rodes, senior (born November 6, 1697), of Hanover County, Virginia, who married Miss Crawford, born 1703. Sarah (Harris) Rodes was the daughter of Robert Harris, of Albemarle, whose will was recorded August 8, 1768. He was the son of William Harris and the grandson of the emigrant, Robert Harris.

Mr. and Mrs. Rodes celebrated their "Golden Wedding" at "Woodlawn," their beautiful home in Madison County, in 1869. Issue:

122.   I. ELIZA RODES, born September 22, 1823; married Robert H. Stone, of Texas.

123. II. SALLY RODES, born September 1, 1825; married John Watson, of Frankfort.

124. III. MARTHA GREEN RODES, born April 9, 1827; married Robert Levi Breck.

125. IV. BELLE RODES, born September 11, 1832; married John Harvie McDowell.

     V. PAULINE CLAY RODES, born June 28, 1838; married Christopher Fields, of Mississippi. No issue.

---

49. Sidney Payne Clay, son of General Green and Sally (Lewis) Clay, was born July 16, 1800, and married (1), September 28, 1822, Nancy B. Keen, who died June 25, 1826, leaving one daughter. Married (2), December 20, 1827, Isabella E. J. Reed, in Nashville, Tennessee. She was born September 13, 1809, and died March 16, 1852. She was the daughter of W. J. Reed and his wife, Margaret Rogers (died August 18, 1835), daughter of John and Sarah (Daugherty) Rogers, of Lunenburg County, Virginia. John Rogers was the son of William Rogers (Test. 1750) and Margaret Caldwell, daughter of John Caldwell, who was born in Ireland and married there Margaret Philips, coming to America after the birth of their fifth child. The Caldwells had gone to Ireland from

Scotland shortly after the Conquest in 1690. Mr. Clay had by his first marriage :

I. SARAH WOOLFOLK CLAY, born March 17, 1824; married Oliver McDowell Keen, March 19, 1843, and died January 28, 1857. Issue :
   I. SIDNEY CLAY KEEN, born March 17, 1844; died December 2, 1873, unmarried.
   II. MARY KEEN, born June 5, 1847; married James T. Shackleford, January 20, 1869. Issue :
      I. W. RODES SHACKLEFORD, born October 26, 1869.
      II. CLAY KEEN SHACKLEFORD, born October 8, 1871.
      III. JOHN HOCKADAY SHACKLEFORD, born December 2, 1873.
      IV. SARAH KEEN SHACKLEFORD, born September 6, 1875.
      V. GEORGE D. SHACKLEFORD, born July 26, 1878; died March 29, 1886.
      VI. JAMES T. SHACKLEFORD, JUNIOR, born December 20, 1880.
      VII. MARY KEEN SHACKLEFORD, born December 19, 1882.

James T. Shackleford is a descendant of George Shackleford (born 1780), youngest son of Colonel Lyne and Elizabeth (Taliaferro) Shackleford, who came to Richmond, Kentucky, from Virginia in 1799. Elizabeth was a sister of Colonel Philip Taliaferro, of "Hockley," and daughter of William Taliaferro, of King and Queen County. Sidney P. Clay had by his second wife :

     I. SIDNEY REED GRUNDY CLAY, born December 20, 1828.

    II. ISABELLA EDWARDS CLAY, born April 12, 1830; died January 13, 1832.

   III. ELIAS DAVIDSON CLAY, born November 29, 1831; died December 6, 1851.

   IV. GREEN CLAY, born December 14, 1833; died May 24, 1860; married Lizzie M. Goodman and left two sons, Sidney D. and Green Clay, both of whom lived to manhood and died unmarried.

Sidney Payne Clay was born at "Whitehall," Madison County, Kentucky, and was graduated from Princeton College, New Jersey. After his marriage he moved to "Escondida," Bourbon County, dying there July 2, 1834. His son, Sidney R. G. Clay, inherited, and until recently has occupied, this beautiful old homestead. He married, in 1867, Sallie Carneal Warfield, daughter of Thomas Barr Warfield (born September 14, 1807), who married, July 17, 1835, Alice Davis Carneal, born May 22, 1817. Issue:

     I. ALICE CARNEAL CLAY; married Captain William Voorhies Judson, United States Army, April 22, 1891. Issue: Sidney Clay Judson, born February 6, 1892.

    II. ISABELLA REED CLAY.

   III. ANNE FIELD CLAY.

   IV. SIDNEY GREEN CLAY; married, December 30, 1896, May Lindsay Stoner, daughter of Colonel Robert Stoner, Confederate States Army, and his wife, Alice Rogers, daughter of Warren B. and Mary Lindsay Rogers, of "Glenwood," and granddaughter of William and Anne Cornick Rogers, of "The Castle," early emigrants to Caneridge from Campbell County, Virginia. Issue: Mary Alice Rogers Clay, born June 20, 1898.

    V. KATE LONGWORTH CLAY.

50. Honorable Brutus J. Clay was born July 1, 1808, in Madison County, Kentucky; educated at Centre College, Danville; settled in Bourbon, where he was prominently interested in agriculture and developing choice breeds of stock. In 1840 he was elected to the legislature; later was President of the Bourbon County Agricultural Association for many years, and did much toward making famous the productions and hospitality of the Bluegrass region. Many remember the active interest of Mr. and Mrs. Clay and their accomplished daughter in the various exhibitions. At that time the president, directors, and other wealthy citizens had cottages upon the grounds, and entertained generously and elegantly the strangers and visitors within their gates. Mr. Clay represented the Ashland District in the Thirty-eighth Congress, where, because of his practical experience and fine judgment, he was made Chairman of the Committee of Agriculture. He was also a member of the Committee on Revolutionary Pensions.

He married (1), February 10, 1835, Amelia Field, born November 2, 1812. She died July 31, 1843, leaving four children. Mr. Clay married (2), November 8, 1844, Anne Field (sister of his first wife), who was born February 12, 1822, and died April 16, 1881. Mr. Clay had issue:

126.   I. MARTHA CLAY, born February 1, 1832.
127.   II. CHRISTOPHER FIELD CLAY, born November 20, 1835.
128.   III. GREEN CLAY, born February 11, 1839.
129.   IV. EZEKIEL FIELD CLAY, born December 1, 1840.
130.   V. CASSIUS M. CLAY, JUNIOR, born March 26, 1846, was the only child by the last wife.

51. General Cassius M. Clay was born October 19, 1810, in Madison County, Kentucky; was educated by private tutors and at Transylvania University, and was graduated from Yale College in 1832; studied law and attended lectures at Transylvania Law School, but never practiced; in 1834 was elected to lower house of legislature from Madison County; re-elected in 1836; removed to Fayette, and represented that county in legislature in 1838–39; was defeated on the slavery issue in the race for re-election; was member of Harrisburg Convention (Whig), 1840, which nominated General Harrison to the Presidency. In 1844 he made an extended tour through the North, advocating the election of his kinsman, Henry Clay; in 1845 edited the "True American," a weekly anti-slavery paper, which, during his illness, was seized by citizens of Lexington, and his entire printing establment shipped to Cincinnati. On the breaking out of the war with Mexico, 1846, he entered service as a captain, and was taken prisoner at Encarnacion in 1847; in 1848 he supported General Taylor; in 1849 became the anti-

17

slavery candidate for Governor, and received four thousand votes; in 1861 was appointed Minister to Russia; was recalled in spring of 1862 and commissioned Major-General of Volunteers, succeeding General Lew Wallace, at Lexington, Kentucky; in 1863 was reappointed Minister to Russia, serving under Presidents Lincoln, Johnson, and Grant until 1867. He was a bold and consistent advocate of emancipation, and this generation can scarcely understand what this meant in Kentucky fifty years ago.

General Clay married, February 18, 1833, Mary Jane Warfield (daughter of Doctor Elisha Warfield and his wife, Maria Barr), a noble, refined woman of broad intellectual attainments, a devoted mother of most worthy children. She was born in Lexington, Kentucky, January 20, 1815. To them were born ten children, of whom Warfield, two sons named Cassius, and Flora died young. The others were:

131.   I. GREEN CLAY, born in 1837.
132.   II. MARY BARR CLAY.
133. III. SARAH LEWIS CLAY.
134.   IV. BRUTUS JUNIUS CLAY, born February 20, 1847.
135.   V. LAURA CLAY.
        VI. ANNIE CLAY, a bright young woman, who went back to the land of "her forefathers" as the wife of Spotswood Dabney Crenshaw, of Richmond, Virginia. Issue: Mary Warfield, Fanny Graves, and Spotswood Dabney Crenshaw, junior.

52. John Clay settled in New Orleans, and married there Julie Duralde, daughter of Martin Duralde, senior, and sister of Martin Duralde, junior, who married the daughter of Henry Clay, of Ashland. The following letter denotes the intimacy of the brothers:

NEW ORLEANS, December 13, 1822.

MY DEAR BROTHER: Mr. Duralde, Susan, and Ann arrived in this city a few days ago in good health. They have done us the pleasure to stay with us while suitable arrangements are established in a home which Mr. Duralde has rented and which is situated in the same street and contiguous to mine. Mrs. Clay seems to be proud of our niece, Ann. We shall both duly appreciate the trust, and we will do all we can to contribute to her amusement and happiness. We regret, most sincerely, the death of our venerable father, Mr. Duralde, senior, of which event you have already been apprised, and that this circumstance should also deprive us from accompanying her to the different amusements offered at this season in our city. I received your letter, per Duralde, of the 8th October, inclosing me certificates of five shares in the United States Bank stock. I thank you for attention to this business. You will have received, some time ago, a Bill of Exchange, to refund you the amount you paid for them.

The suit of Smith against myself, which has been a long time hanging over my head, was decided on yesterday, to my great mortification and disappointment, in the United States Debtors Court of this city. The conduct of Judge Dick was marked with hostility against me in the whole pleading, and, particularly in the charge he gave the jury, he evinced evident partiality. I have appealed to the United States Court at

Washington. It is possible it may be called for February term. If so, I wish you to attend to it, and get some eminent lawyer to join you. If it should be for January term, 1824, I have engaged Mr. Livingston to assist you; his acquaintance with the laws and usages of this country, joined with his eminent talents, would benefit my case. I will allow you five hundred dollars for your attention to this business, and, in the event of success, two thousand dollars. I could not pay you immediately, but rest assured I will so soon as I can conveniently. For the other attorney, you will endeavor to procure one on reasonable terms. Should this suit go against me, I am paralyzed for the rest of my life. I already begin to feel the loss of credit here. By getting a successful issue, I am confident that in a few years I'll be able to pay all my debts, and I could do it in that way not to be felt, and at the same time preserve my credit. There is so much justice on my part, and so much injustice on the other hand to decide against me, that I still have hopes of a favorable decision. Mr. H. Johnson and J. S. Johnson, delegates from this country, to whom I have communicated freely, will furnish considerable information in my case. I will, however, in a few days, make you a statement of the circumstances attending my bankruptcy, and forward to you at Washington. I regret not being able to loan you the five thousand dollars. I have not got over the embarrassment occasioned by my building. My last season was not so productive as formerly. I have also met with some losses; add to these the most distressing times. Short crops and decline in prices, at heavy pressure for funds, pervades our country.

Julie joins me in our best wishes for yourself, Mrs. Clay, and family.   Your affectionate brother,

JOHN CLAY.

53. Henry Clay, the Hero of the Clan, the great Kentuckian, and the greater American, was born in Hanover County, Virginia, April 12, 1777. All are familiar with his life from the day on which he earned the soubriquet of "The Mill-boy of the Slashes" until his remains were laid to rest in the vaulted chamber of the imposing monument Kentucky has erected to his memory. We can speak no word of eulogy that has not been already spoken, for historians have vied with each other in computing the wonderful results of his great moral and intellectual achievements, but probably the most salient points of his successful career, at least those which Mr. Clay desired most should be remembered, are to be found engraved upon the large gold medal presented him by the citizens of New York in commemoration of his National service. The inscription, about which he was consulted, reads thus:

SENATE, 1806.
SPEAKER, 1811.
WAR WITH GREAT BRITAIN, 1812.
GHENT, 1814.
SPANISH AMERICA, 1821.
MISSOURI COMPROMISE, 1821.
AMERICAN SYSTEM, 1824.
GREECE, 1824.
SECRETARY OF STATE, 1825.
PANAMA INSTRUCTIONS, 1826.
TARIFF COMPROMISE, 1833.
PUBLIC DOMAIN, 1833 – 1841.
PEACE WITH FRANCE PRESERVED, 1835.
COMPROMISE, 1850.

This inscription indicates the work he had satisfactorily accomplished in the half century of his public service, and near the end of life he placed upon it the signet of his approbation.

His integrity as a public man remained without blemish throughout his long political career, and almost every thing he did was illumined by a grand conception of the destinies of his country, a glowing national spirit, and a lofty patriotism.

Mr. Clay died in Washington City, June 29, 1852, in the seventy-sixth year of his age. On July 1st the members of the Senate and House of Representatives, together with the city authorities, military companies, and civic associations, accompanied his remains from the National Hotel to the Senate Chamber, where, attended by the President of the United States, the Cabinet, and the officers of the Army and Navy, the funeral services took place. The remains were then brought to Kentucky, the funeral cortege passing through Baltimore, Wilmington, Philadelphia, the principal places of New Jersey and New York, Cleveland, Cincinnati, Louisville, and then to Lexington. Everywhere the people assembled by thousands to pay the last tribute of respect to the illustrious statesman. From his own beautiful home the "Sage of Ashland" was carried to his last resting-place. He married, in 1799, Lucretia Hart, born March 18, 1781, daughter of Thomas Hart and Susanna Gray, who settled in Lexington, Kentucky, in 1794. Mrs. Clay survived him twelve years, and sleeps by his side in the second sarcophagus in the tomb. Mrs. Clay was a gentle, sweet woman, and while she spent much of her time with her husband in Washington, she cared little for the social life of the Capital. During her stay there, while Mr. Clay was Secretary of State, she lost two lovely daughters, Eliza, who died en route to Washington, and Mrs. Duralde, who died with yellow fever in New Orleans.

At the end of President Adams' administration she returned to Ashland, never to leave it again. Another, and her last daughter, Mrs. Erwin, died, and Theodore, her eldest son, was hopelessly insane. From these sorrows she never recovered, and spent her time in the seclusion of her family, receiving only her most intimate friends. Mr. and Mrs. Clay had issue:

I. HENRIETTA CLAY; died young.

II. THEODORE WYTHE CLAY, born in 1802; received, when a mere lad, a blow upon his head, which fractured his skull. It was trepanned by Doctor Pindell, a surgeon of the Revolution, who expressed the fear that, at or about the time he reached manhood, he would become insane. This fear was realized, and he died, at an advanced age, at the Asylum for the Insane, at Lexington, Kentucky. His boyhood gave exceeding promise of brilliant attainment.

136. III. THOMAS HART CLAY, born 1803; died 1871.
    IV. SUSAN HART CLAY, born 1805; married, April 22, 1822, Martin Duralde, of New Orleans, and had two sons, Martin and Henry Clay Duralde. Both died in early manhood, unmarried.
137. V. ANN BROWN CLAY, born April 7, 1807; died in 1835.
    VI. LUCRETIA HART CLAY, born in 1809.
138. VII. HENRY CLAY, JUNIOR, born in 1811; was killed in the war with Mexico.
    VIII. ELIZA CLAY, born 1815; died in Lebanon, Ohio, in 1825, while en route to Washington with her parents. But a few years since her remains were brought to Lexington and interred in the family lot at the cemetery.
    IX. LAURA CLAY, born 1815; died in infancy.
139. X. JAMES BROWN CLAY, born November, 1817, in Washington City; died in Montreal, Canada, January 26, 1864.
    XI. JOHN MORRISON CLAY, born 1821; died 1887. In 1866 he married Mrs. Josephine Erwin, nee Russell. No issue. Mrs. Clay lives on a part of the Ashland estate, and since the death of her husband has managed the farm and thoroughbred stock most successfully. She possesses a decided literary taste, and all spare time is devoted to writing.

54. Clement Claiborne Clay was a member of the Alabama Legislature; Judge of the Court of Madison County; elected to the United States Senate when only thirty-five years old (and that after a defeat for Congress a short time before), and re-elected, without opposition, a second term. He resigned his seat in United States Congress in 1861, and was elected Senator by First Confederate Congress; was offered, but declined, office of Judge Advocate General for Alabama by Presi-

dent Jefferson Davis ; was Commissioner, with Honorable Jacob Thompson, to Canada on a secret mission in behalf of the Southern Confederacy ; returned to the South in 1865, just before the close of hostilities; was shipwrecked off Charleston Harbor, and narrowly escaped drowning. Mr. Clay had made all arrangements for leaving the country at the close of the war, when, at Lagrange, Georgia, he read a proclamation charging him with complicity in the assassination of President Lincoln, and offering one hundred thousand dollars reward for his arrest. Indignant and horrified at such an accusation, he, against the remonstrances of his friends, surrendered himself to the nearest Federal Officer, General Wilson, at Macon, Georgia. He was taken to Savannah, Georgia, and, with his gifted and devoted wife and President Davis and family, was carried to Fortress Monroe, May, 1865, and there incarcerated until May, 1866, when, through the influence of prominent officials, among them General U. S. Grant, and the importunities of his wife, he was released by President Andrew Johnson. The case against him never came to trial. The charges were utterly false. He died in Madison County, Alabama, in 1882. He married Virginia Caroline Tunstall February 1, 1843. Left no issue.

55. John Withers Clay was born January 11, 1820, and married, November 11, 1847, Mary Fenwick Lewis, daughter of John Heywood Lewis. Issue :

     I. CARALIZA CLAY.
    II. JOHN WITHERS CLAY; married Mary, daughter of Rolf
        Saunders.
   III. CLEMENT C. CLAY.
   IV. CLARENCE H. CLAY.
    V. ELLEN L. CLAY.
   VI. WILLIAM L. CLAY.
  VII. MARY LEWIS CLAY.
 VIII. SUSANNA W. CLAY.
   IX. VIRGINIA C. CLAY.
    X. ELODIE CLAY.

These were all born at Huntsville, Alabama. The father was paralyzed in 1885, when his daughters, Virginia and Susanna W., took charge of the Huntsville Democrat, which they have conducted successfully to the present time. None of the girls are married, but are busily devoting themselves to their chosen work, and lovingly caring for their aged parents.

William Lewis Clay was admitted to the bar in 1873; elected City Attorney in 1875, and is now practicing law at Huntsville, Alabama. He married Louisa, daughter of Doctor James T. Johnson, of Frederick County, Maryland, October, 1878. No issue.

56. Mary Sledge Greene, born August 17, 1827; died July 13, 1881; married, December 1, 1840, Allison Nelson, born March 17, 1823, and died October 7, 1862. Issue:

140.   I. EMMA CYNTHIA NELSON, born November 24, 1842.
141.   II. ALICE SOPHIA NELSON, born April 26, 1845.
142.   III. JOHN ALSTON NELSON, born July 22, 1848; died June 21, 1891.

---

57. Clement Comer Clay Greene, First Lieutenant, Cobb's Cavalry, Civil War, 1861–65; married (1), April 25, 1850, Mary Frances Goodwin, born October 17, 1833, died April 17, 1871. Issue:

143.   I. ALSTON HUNTER GREENE, born February 9, 1851.
144.   II. WILLIAM DANIEL GREENE, born October 8, 1852.
        III. JULIA ELIZABETH GREENE, born March 1, 1855.
145.   IV. CLEMENT CLAY GREENE, JUNIOR, born October 7, 1857.
        V. ALLISON NELSON GREENE, born April 9, 1860.
146.   VI. ANNA BLANCHE GREENE, born June 18, 1863.
147.   VII. MARY FRANCES GREENE, born January 9, 1867.
        VIII. ROBERT LEE GREENE, born March 21, 1870; died April 28, 1872.

          Clement Comer Clay Greene married (2) Louisa Wilson, born February 26, 1850. Issue:

        IX. EDNA EARLE GREENE, born July 18, 1873; married, August 16, 1892, William Douglas Brannan, born July 22, 1870. Issue: Nell and Mary Greene Brannan.
        X. FOREST GREENE, born May 27, 1877.
        XI. HUBERT GREENE, born August 7, 1880.

58. William Augustine Greene was married in 1853 to Louisa Susan Pitman.   Issue :

148.   I. MARY EMMA GREENE, born November 9, 1854; died November 14, 1892.

149.   II. ALLISON LAWSON GREENE, born November 27, 1855; died June 3, 1893.

        III. WILLIAM AUGUSTINE GREENE, JUNIOR, born August 26, 1858; married, November 11, 1879, Margaret W. Thompson. Issue : William E., Lamar, and Marion E. Greene.

        IV. ANNIE LAURIE GREENE, born May 3, 1857 ; died August 3, 1886; married, November 22, 1877, Thomas Henry Jeffries, born April 16, 1854. Issue : Maybelle M., Werner Moore, Clymer DeF., and Susan A. Jeffries.

59. Cordelia E. Greene married, August 16, 1857, Henry Holcombe Glenn, born January 9, 1829 ; died November 10, 1883. Issue : Thomas Cobb, Henry H., Henry Luther, Mary Kate, and Robert M. Glenn.

60. Alexander Bruce, born September 5, 1797 ; died April 18, 1851 ; married, February 18, 1819, Amanda M. Bragg, in Lewis County.   Issue :

        I. JOHN LOGAN BRUCE; married Henrietta Abbott, of an old New Jersey family. Issue : Minnie and Alice Bruce.

        II. THOMAS J. BRUCE; married Mary Abbott, sister of Henrietta. Issue : Henry Clay, Malcolm, Robert, Henrietta, and Corinne Bruce.

        III. HENRY CLAY BRUCE; married Mary Conner. Issue : Sidney, Mary, Thomas, Samuel, William, and John Bruce.

IV. BRUNETTE PROCTOR BRUCE; married Captain Thomas E.
Redden. Issue: James, Elizabeth Clay, Thomas,
Harvey Lewis, Bruce, Belville Moss, Henry Clay,
and Lucy Blakemore Redden.
V. NANCY BURNEY BRUCE; married William Elliott. Issue:
Brunette, Isabella, Octavia, Amanda, Lelia, Lucy,
Edna, William, Thomas, Alexander Bruce, Henry
Clay, and Mary Washington Elliott.
VI. LUCY A. BRUCE; married Doctor Samuel Ellis. Issue:
Elizabeth Clay, Thomas Walker, and Samuel Ellis.
VII. ALEXANDER BRUCE; died young.
VIII. SUSAN M. BRUCE; died young.
150. IX. HORATIO WASHINGTON BRUCE, born February 22, 1830.

---

61. James Mitchell Clay, of Plattsburg, Missouri, was
born in 1824, in Kentucky, and moved to Missouri in
1839; settled in Clay County; married (1) Mary C.
Gordon, daughter of Thomas C. and Charlotte (Grigsby)
Gordon. Issue:

I. WILLIAM CLAY; married Miss Hockaday.
II. EMMA CLAY; married Fred Essex.
III. SALLIE CLAY; married Charles Fergerson.
IV. HENRY R. CLAY; married Victoria Stoddard.
James M. Clay married (2) Alice Price. Issue:
V. JAMES MITCHELL CLAY, JUNIOR.

---

62. Nancy Finch, born 1788; married, in 1810, Zephaniah Robnett, and died in 1838. Issue:

I. SAMUEL ROBNETT, born 1811; married Mary Ritchie.
II. LUCINDA GREEN ROBNETT, born 1812.
III. HENRY ROBNETT, born 1814.
IV. RACHEL POVALL ROBNETT, born 1815; married Aaron
Bright in 1834, and died in 1860.

V. John T. Robnett, born 1818; married in Texas. Issue.

VI. Edward Robnett, born 1820; died in 1838.

VII. Rebecca A. Robnett, born 1822; married (1), in 1856,
Charles Lander; (2), in 1875, Joseph Tureman, and
resides in Carlisle, Kentucky.

VIII. George Robnett, born 1824; died in 1844.

IX. Mary Clay Robnett; married Robert Bradley.

X. Sarah Robnett; married Thomas Menefee.

---

63. Henry Finch married Cynthia Collier. Issue:

I. John Finch.

II. Lucy Green Finch; married Adam Styres Hibler. Issue:

    I. Henry Finch Hibler; married Mary Brindley.
Issue: William F., Harvey, Bishop, Eddie,
and Henry Hibler.

    II. Emily Hibler; married W. A. Parker, of Paris.
Kentucky. Issue: Harry S. and W. A.
Parker, junior.

    III. Cynthia Hibler; married D. P. Robb, a banker
at Versailles, Kentucky.

    IV. Sallie Hibler; married (1) James Abbott, who
left a son, French Abbott; (2) B. F. Pullen.

    V. Joseph Hibler; died unmarried.

    VI. Thomas Hibler; died unmarried.

    VII. Lavinia Hibler; married Reverend Benjamin
Ricketts. Issue: Abbott, Roy, and Nell Ricketts.

    VIII. Mary Edna Hibler; died young and unmarried.

    IX. J. Harvey Hibler, of Paris, Kentucky.

    X. Lucy Hibler; married (1) W. R. Proctor, of
Mammoth Cave; (2) R. S. Starks, of Midway,
Kentucky. Issue: W. R. Proctor and Mary
Edna, James S., and Katherine Poynter Starks.

64. Henry C. Clay married, September 5, 1816, Mary Grimes. Issue:

    I. CHARLES CLAY; died unmarried.

    II. NANCY CLAY; died unmarried.

    III. SAMUEL H. CLAY; married Julia, daughter of Captain Washington and Elizabeth (Bedford) Kennedy. Issue:

        I. ANNIE CLAY; married William Pierce. Issue: Elizabeth, William, Julia, Laura, Frank, May, and John Pierce.

        II. WASHINGTON CLAY; married Sophia Drake, and lives in Illinois. Issue: Harry, Minnie, and Edgar Clay.

        III. HARRY C. CLAY; married Jennie Grimes. Issue: Ernest Clay; died young and unmarried.

        IV. MATTIE CLAY; married William Lair. No issue.

        V. CHARLES CLAY; married (1) Lydia Grimes; (2) Mary Tribble. No issue.

        VI. MARGARET CLAY; married Robert Ferguson. No issue.

        VII. REVEREND FRANK CLAY; married Mittie Grimes. Issue: Samuel Clay.

        VIII. REVEREND SAMUEL CLAY; married ———. No issue.

    IV. JANE CLAY; married Aris Talbot in 1838, and died 1852. Issue: Samuel, Jane, Annie (married Hector Lewis, of Arkansas. Issue: Mattie), William H., Benjamin A., of Oklahoma, and Mrs. John Sturgel.

---

65. Letitia Clay, daughter of Samuel and Nancy (Winn) Clay; married, May 10, 1810, Edward B. Moran, son of William Moran (born November 23, 1748) and his wife, Rebecca Barber Moran, born February 22, 1748. Issue:

151.   I. CAROLINE B. MORAN; married Benjamin C. Bedford.
           (See 80.)
152. II. NANCY A. MORAN; married Nathaniel P. Rogers.
153. III. REBECCA BARBER MORAN; married Samuel Hedges.
154. IV. ELIZABETH JANE MORAN; married Harvey A. Rogers.
       V. LETITIA MORAN, born February 26, 1821; died young and
           unmarried.
      VI. HENRIETTA MORAN, born March 28, 1823; died young.
     VII. YOUNG W. MORAN, born April 17, 1823; married, July 6,
           1853, Susan King, daughter of Captain John and Sally
           (King) Bedford. Issue: Edward B. and Sallie K.
           Moran, who married Frank Clay. Issue.

66. George Clay, son of Samuel and Nancy (Winn)
Clay; married, November 6, 1817, Almira Bainbridge,
and had issue. Of these :

  I. WILLIAM CLAY; married his cousin, Elizabeth Clay, daugh-
     ter of Colonel Littleberry and Arabella Maccoun Clay,
     and died soon after without issue.
 II. LITTLEBERRY CLAY, born in Bourbon County, Kentucky,
     October 21, 1820, and moved with his parents to
     Warren County, Missouri, in 1821. His father, George
     Clay, was a man of wealth and position, owning and
     running several fine boats on the Missouri and Missis-
     sippi rivers. He lived at St. Louis; died there in
     1858, aged seventy years. His wife died some years
     before. Littleberry Clay, during 1865 and 1866, ran
     the "Cornelia" to New Orleans. He moved to Lewis
     County, Missouri, in 1866, and married Barbara David-
     son, an adopted daughter of William Jones, of St.
     Louis. Six of their nine children are living, viz:
     Amanda, Oliver C. (prosecuting attorney of Monti-
     cello, Lewis County, Missouri), Thomas L., S. W., Ella,
     and James H. Clay.

General GREEN CLAY.　　　　General CASSIUS MARCELLUS CLAY.

67. Littleberry Bedford Clay was born in Bourbon County February 13, 1799, and died in Lexington, August 5, 1879. He was married in January, 1817, when the united ages of himself and wife were scarcely thirty-four years. His first wife was Arabella Anne Tilford Maccoun, daughter of James Maccoun (1767–1832) and his wife, Elizabeth Rice (1774–1833), who were married in Mercer County, Kentucky, October 21, 1797. Elizabeth Rice was the daughter of Reverend David Rice, born in Hanover County, Virginia, December 20, 1733, and died in Green County, Kentucky, June 18, 1816, and his wife, Mary, daughter of Reverend Samuel Blair, of Faggs Manor, Pennsylvania. James Maccoun was the son of James Maccoun, junior, and grandson of James Maccoun, senior, of the McAfee Company, early pioneers of Kentucky.

Littleberry B. Clay was a man of fine physique and courtly manners. He entered the Confederate Army at sixty-three years of age, and served during the war. He enlisted as a private, and rose to the rank of Colonel; was a member of General Raines' Staff, General Price's Division, Trans-Mississippi Department. At his death, in August, 1879, the following notice appeared in the Lexington Observer and Reporter, written by Colonel John O. Hodges, a comrade in arms:

"Colonel Littleberry Bedford Clay, Confederate States Army, died in this city Monday night, at the residence of his son, Samuel Clay, junior, in the eighty-first year of his age.

"Colonel Clay was a native of Bourbon County, Kentucky, but for many years before the war lived in Cass County, Missouri. There, under the call of the Governor of the State, in June, 1861, he took the musket of a private soldier, and did brave and generous duty throughout the longest and most arduous service of the late civil war. At Independence, Missouri, June 17th, he stood in the front ranks, and was among the first to advance when General Marmaduke gave the command. Again at Camp Cole, the next day, he was to be found in the lead. In this way he followed the fortunes of Marmaduke, General Joe Shelby, Sterling Price, General Raines, and Kirby Smith to the end of the war, and was among the last to lay down his arms when peace was declared. Four times during Missouri's desperate struggles was he wounded, and that seriously. During the contest around the fortifications of Lexington, lasting from September 12th to the 20th, he was ever in the front, and there received a dangerous wound in the head. Two days before he had been wounded in the leg, but not so seriously as to keep him from the front. At Carthage and at Wilson's Creek he was in the thickest of the fray, and was not a hundred yards from the spot where General Lyons fell. At Pea Ridge he was again wounded, but not so seriously as at Lexington. Those who stood by him in the field, and those who knew him in camp, with one accord agree to both his courage and his generosity, and many a brave heart will be pained by the information of his death. His remains will be taken to the family burying-grounds in Bourbon County to-day for interment. Peace to his ashes."

Colonel Clay had five children by his first wife, the youngest dying in infancy. Mrs. Clay was an accomplished and beautiful woman. She died May 30, 1828, in Bourbon County, leaving four small children, viz :

155. I. HENRY CLAY, born 1819, of Hendricks County, Indiana.
156. II. OLIVIA MACCOUN CLAY, born January 13, 1823.
157. III. SAMUEL CLAY, JUNIOR, born April 19, 1825.
158. IV. ELIZABETH RICE CLAY, born in 1826.

Colonel Clay married (2) Almira Dudley April 22, 1830. No issue. He married (3), in 1838, Amanda Moore, daughter of Andrew and Sally (Morin) Moore and granddaughter of Captain William Moore, a Revolutionary soldier and an early emigrant to Kentucky. Captain Moore died in November, 1829, and was buried at Cynthiana with military honors. He was the personal friend of General Lafayette. Captain Moore was the first Clerk of the Court of Quarter Sessions and of the Circuit Court of Harrison County, and these positions were held by himself and sons, Andrew and Henry Coleman Moore, from 1792 to 1832, a period of forty years. Colonel and Amanda (Moore) Clay had issue :

I. ANDREW MOORE CLAY ; married Carrie, a daughter of Higgins Chinn. Issue :
    I. AMANDA MOORE CLAY ; married James Monroe Brannin, of Fort Worth, Texas. Issue : Lucile.
    II. CAROLINE B. CLAY ; married John C. Cushwa. Issue.

III. SAMUEL HIGGINS CLAY.
IV. FRANKIE RIVERS CLAY; married Harry Slater.
Issue.
V. HATTIE PROCTOR CLAY.
VI. MAYBELLE CLAY.
VII. JOHN ROLAND CLAY.
VIII. JAMES HENRY CLAY.
Andrew M. Clay was a soldier in the Confederate Army.
II. LITTLEBERRY CLAY, a Southern soldier; died in prison during the Civil War in Missouri.
III. WILLIAM L. CLAY was born in 1843, and served in the Confederate Army; was married four times. Issue: Katie, Brutus, and Harry Clay.
IV. HATTIE A. CLAY, the worthy daughter of a good mother.

68. Richard Clay, of Bourbon County, married Olivia Parsons February 5, 1840. Issue: George, and Clara, who married —— Ewing, and died, leaving a daughter, now of age, living with relatives in Tennessee.

69. John Clay married, first, Eliza Ward (sister of Almanza Ward, of Winchester, Kentucky); second, Miss Reese, of Georgia. Issue:

159. I. JOHN WARD CLAY, of Mt. Sterling, Kentucky.
160. II. SAMUEL E. CLAY, of Montgomery County, Kentucky.
III. SARAH CLAY; married and moved to Illinois.
IV. WILLIAM CLAY.

70. Rachel Clay married Robert McCoun, of Lexington, of the Salt River, Mercer County, family, and bore him two children, Nancy and John. Nancy mar-

ried Willis Talbott November 26, 1840, and moved to Hendricks County, Indiana. John died unmarried.

------

71. William Green Clay married Patsy P. Bedford. (See page 96.)

------

72. Benjamin F. Bedford, senior, of Bourbon County, born May, 1799, married, January 27, 1819, Eleanor G. Buckner, born November 2, 1799. Issue :

> I. ELIZABETH H. BEDFORD, born November 12, 1819; died January 28, 1845.
> II. BENJAMIN T. BEDFORD, born March 19, 1821; married, November 27, 1849, Mary Ellen, daughter of George Parker and Lucy Donaldson, daughter of Colonel Donaldson, of the War of 1812. George P. was son of Captain Thomas and Mary (Taylor) Parker, of Snow Hill, Maryland. Benjamin T. and Mary E. Bedford had issue: Sidney Bedford; married Miss Harper and lives in Franklin County.
> III. JOHN C. BEDFORD, born November 17, 1822.
> IV. MARY A. BEDFORD, born September 22, 1824.
> 161. V. HARRY P. BEDFORD, born April 10, 1826.
> VI. STEPHEN BEDFORD, born January 17, 1829.
> VII. SARAH E. BEDFORD, born November 25, 1830.
> VIII. FRANKLIN BEDFORD, born August 29, 1833.
> IX. HILLARY BEDFORD, born August 15, 1835.
> X. ALEXANDER HAWES BEDFORD, born March, 1838; married, November 29, 1869, Ida R., daughter of Sampson D. and Sarah Stemmons Talbott. Issue: Dousie P. Bedford.

------

73. Rachel Dawson married Rezin H. Gist in 1812. He was born in Baltimore in 1797, and died in 1834;

was a Captain of Kentucky troops in the War of 1812; was the son of Captain David Gist and his wife, Rebecca Hammond, daughter of Rezin Hammond, of Millersville, Maryland. Rezin H. Gist was the nephew of General Mordecai Gist, an aide to General Washington, and great-nephew of Colonel Christopher Gist, of colonial times. The Gist and Hammond families were early settlers in Maryland, wealthy and prominent, and traced their lineage, through English ancestry, to Cromwell's time. Issue:

162. I. ANNA GIST, born 1817; married, 1834, David Howell, of Clark County, Kentucky.

II. SUSAN GIST, born 1824; married Leander M. Cox. No issue.

163. III. RACHEL E. GIST, born 1826; married James H. Turner.

164. IV. HENRIETTA CLAY GIST, born 1828; married (1) Hiram Wilson, son of Henry Wilson and his wife, Henrietta Parker (born December 20, 1793; died July 1, 1870), daughter of Captain Thomas and Mary (Taylor) Parker, of Snow Hill, Maryland; (2) Thomas H. Fox. Issue: Hiram Wilson, Susan Gist Fox, and Eliza Bell Fox, who married John C. Rogers, of Fayette County. Issue: William and Thomas Hunton Rogers.

---

74. Henrietta Dawson married James Prewitt. Issue, twelve children:

I. HENRY CLAY PREWITT; married Elizabeth Meteer. Issue: Martha Clay Prewitt, who married Doctor M. S. Browne, of Winchester, Kentucky. Issue: Henry Prewitt Browne.

165. II. PATSY CHANDLER PREWITT.

III. ROBERT PREWITT.

IV. THOMAS PREWITT ; died young.

V. JOSIAH PREWITT ; died young.

VI. EMILY PREWITT ; died young.

VII. JAMES PREWITT ; died young.

166. VIII. CASWELL PREWITT.

167. IX. ALLEN G. PREWITT.

168. X. CLIFTON PREWITT.

XI. MARY PREWITT ; married N. B. Young, of Mt. Sterling, Kentucky. Issue : James Prewitt Young, born August, 1872.

XII. JOHN T. PREWITT ; married (1) Wenona Wilson. Issue : Eva Clay Prewitt ; (2) Elizabeth Reid. He died April, 1894.

---

75. Elizabeth Bedford, daughter of Littleberry and Mattie Clay Bedford, born December 7, 1794 ; married Captain Washington Kennedy June 25, 1812. He was born June 25, 1779, and commanded a company in the War of 1812. Was son of John Kennedy, a Revolutionary soldier who settled on Kennedy's Creek in 1779. Issue :

I. JULIA KENNEDY ; married Samuel H. Clay. (See 64.)

169. II. MATTIE KENNEDY ; married Charles Garrard.

III. MARY KENNEDY.

170. IV. PATSY KENNEDY.

V. LITTLEBERRY KENNEDY.

VI. JOHN B. KENNEDY, born December 1, 1824 ; married, November, 1845, Mary M., daughter of Jesse and Polly (Waugh) Kennedy. Issue :

I. SIDNEY B. KENNEDY ; married Fannie Miller, daughter of James Miller, of "Sunny Side."

II. MARY J. KENNEDY ; married Thompson Tarr.

(John B. Kennedy married (2) Mrs. Alice Redmond, daughter of Greenberry Dorsey, of Louisiana. No issue.)

76. Littleberry Bedford, born July 30, 1798, died January 23, 1880; married Cicely Rollins, born January 30, 1798, died in 1843.   Issue:

> I. LITTLEBERRY BEDFORD, born February, 1821; married, December, 1873, Fannie Horton, daughter of Memuca and Claramond (Harvey) Horton, of Georgia.
> II. ELIZABETH BEDFORD; married Smith Lindsay.
> III. MARY BEDFORD; married James C. Garrard, of Pendleton County.
> IV. CAROLINE BEDFORD; married Samuel Pryor.   Issue.
> V. THOMAS F. BEDFORD, of Missouri.
> VI. WILLIAM P. BEDFORD.
> VII. WEBSTER C. BEDFORD.

---

77. Captain John Bedford married Sally King.   Issue:

> I. LITTLEBERRY MOSELY BEDFORD, born July 26, 1823; married, January 12, 1848, Mary A. Smith (born May 16, 1823), daughter of George A. and Elizabeth Edwards Smith, and granddaughter of Withers Smith and Jane Lane, his wife, who was the daughter of James and Lydia Lane, and granddaughter of William Lane (who died in Westmoreland in 1760) and wife, Martha Lane. Issue: Sallie Bedford; married Joseph E. Hegdes.
> II. SUSAN BEDFORD.   (See 65).
> III. JOHN BEDFORD; married Emma L., daughter of Charles P. Shire, of Charleston, South Carolina.   Issue:
>> I. CHARLES W. BEDFORD; married Blanche Dorriss. Issue: Emma R., Florence, Susie, and Charles Bedford.
>> II. MARY BEDFORD.
>> III. SUSAN BEDFORD.
>> IV. JOHN M. BEDFORD.
>> V. WILLIAM BEDFORD; married Lutie Collier, of Millersburg.
>> VI. SALLIE BEDFORD; married W. L. Adams.

VII. MATTIE BEDFORD ; married C. E. Moore. Issue :
Eugene and Clarence.
VIII. LITTLEBERRY BEDFORD ; married Ella Chansler.
Issue : Emma.
IX. EDWARD BEDFORD ; married Matty Kenny, of Cane-
ridge.

---

78. Augustine Volney Bedford, born August 18, 1802 ;
married Elizabeth Lewis, daughter of General James and
granddaughter of Governor Garrard, of Kentucky. She
died August 24, 1873. Issue :

I. WILLIAM G. BEDFORD ; died young.
II. M. CORDELIA BEDFORD ; married O. V. Talbott. No issue.
171. III. JAMES G. BEDFORD, of Monroe County, Missouri.
172. IV. JEPTHA D. BEDFORD, born December 12, 1837.
V. LITTLEBERRY BEDFORD, of Denver, Colorado.
173. VI. SALLY MARIA BEDFORD, died December 2, 1885.
VII. BENJAMIN F. BEDFORD, of Mansfield, Illinois ; married N.
E. Jacoby. Issue : Mary C., James, Ernest, and Lallah
Bedford.
VIII. STEPHEN GARRARD BEDFORD ; married Amanda Jacoby.
Issue : Clifton C. and Walter and Nellie Bedford.

---

80. Benjamin C. Bedford, born August 17, 1807 ; married (1) Caroline B. Moran, born February 29, 1812. Issue :
Two sons. Married (2) Ann Maria Garrard, daughter of
General James and Nancy Lewis Garrard, and granddaughter of Governor Garrard, of Kentucky, who bore
him six children. He had :

I. EDWARD BEDFORD ; died young.
174. II. BENJAMIN F. BEDFORD, born August 23, 1830 ; died in 1897.

20

III. JEPTHA GARRARD BEDFORD, born September 24, 1836; married Mattie E. Baker.

175. IV. NANCY LEWIS BEDFORD, born May 8, 1838.

176. V. MARGARET T. BEDFORD, born March 4, 1840.

VI. JAMES GARRARD BEDFORD, born December 25, 1842; died
October 14, 1862.

VII. THOMAS BEDFORD, born January 17, 1845; married, September 14, 1869, Mary Emmon, and lives in Monroe
County, Missouri.

VIII. ALPHEUS LEWIS BEDFORD, born February 17, 1848; married Margaret A., daughter of Green and Caroline Bedford, of Bourbon, September 14, 1868. Lives in Chick-
asaw Nation, Indian Territory.

81. Archibald M. Bedford, of Bourbon County, born
February 25, 1812; died September 12, 1860; married
Elizabeth Hawes Bedford. Issue :

I. AYLETTE BEDFORD, died young.

II. ELLEN BEDFORD; married William Bedford, of Boone
County, Missouri.

III. THOMAS A. BEDFORD; died in the Confederate Army, a
member of the First Kentucky Battalion of Mounted
Infantry.

IV. JOHN C. BEDFORD, born January 20, 1843; married, August
18, 1865, Louisa, daughter of James and Alvira (Sparks)
Huffstetter. He was a Southern soldier, serving faith-
fully until the close of the war. Issue : Frank, Mary,
Mattie, Maggie, Alvira, and James.

V. ARCHIBALD W. BEDFORD, born January 14, 1845; was a
soldier in the Confederate Army. He married, November
1, 1865, Henrietta, daughter of John and Martha (Prewitt)
Goff. Issue : John, Mattie, and Caswell Prewitt.

82. Edwin G. Bedford, born August 27, 1814; married
(1) Margaret, daughter of General James Garrard and his
wife, Nancy Lewis, daughter of Thomas Lewis (born May

8, 1749) and his wife, Elizabeth Payne. Thomas Lewis was the son of Stephen and Elizabeth (Offutt) Lewis. Mr. Bedford married (2) Lucy DeGraftenried. Issue: E. G. Bedford, junior; married Ellen L. Matthews. Issue: Edwin Matthews and Elizabeth Gist Bedford.

---

83. Henry Clay, the fifth of that name in direct descent, was born June 4, 1798. In 1821 he married Olivia, daughter of Major George M. and Henrietta (Clay) Bedinger. Issue: A son, who with his mother died in 1823. In 1826 Mr. Clay married (2) Elizabeth, daughter of Samuel and Elizabeth (Cunningham) Scott. Issue: Five children, three of whom reached maturity. In 1837 Mr. Clay married (3) Mary, daughter of George and Ellis Chadwell, of Jessamine County. Issue: Six children, of whom two are now living:

    I. SAMUEL SCOTT CLAY; married, April 17, 1849, Katherine, daughter of Henry C. and Lucy (Ware) Bedford. Issue: Six children, of whom Lucy, Elizabeth, Henry, Frank, Margaret Helm, and William reached maturity. Of these, only three are living:

        I. HENRY CLAY; married Helen, daughter of Doctor David and Hannah (Cooke) Keller.

        II. FRANK CLAY; married Sallie Moran. (See 65.)

        III. MARGARET HELM CLAY; married Henry Clay, son of Henry C. and Elizabeth P. (Lewis) Howard.

    II. MARGARET HELM CLAY; married Edward P. Kelly, of Philadelphia; died without issue.

    III. JOSEPH HELM CLAY.

    IV. GEORGE CLAY.

    V. LETITIA CLAY.

Joseph Helm, George, and Letitia Clay are unmarried, and reside upon the old homestead, where their father died on June 20, 1890. Joseph Helm and George Clay were Union soldiers under their uncle, Captain M. M. Clay, Company C, Twenty-first Kentucky Infantry. Are Republicans.

84. John Clay, born February 15, 1800, died December 5, 1876; married, October 9, 1823, Nancy Blanton, born August 14, 1806. Issue:

> I. HARRISON BLANTON CLAY, born March 24, 1825; married Bettie Gass December 6, 1888; died 1898.
> II. SALLIE CLAY, born May 12, 1827; died July 17, 1888; married Henri Gaitskill. Issue:
>> I. CLAY GAITSKILL; married Leah W. Harp.
>> II. HENRY GAITSKILL; married Elizabeth Harp.
>> III. MARGARET GAITSKILL; married Silas Bedford. Issue: Sarah Louise Bedford.
> III. MARGARET ELIZABETH CLAY, born December 15, 1828; died August 19, 1871.
> IV. HENRIETTA POVALL CLAY, born December 25, 1830; died April 11, 1845.
> V. RICHARD HENRY CLAY, born April 5, 1832; died January 14, 1835.
> VI. JOHN CARTER CLAY, born November 11, 1834; married Laura Hume. Issue:
>> I. M. H. CLAY; married Mary W. Thomas. Issue: James and Laura Clay.
>> II. HARRY B. CLAY; married Maggie Turney October 29, 1890.
>> III. J. FRANK CLAY; married Lucille Turney December 9, 1891.
> VII. SYTHE BLANTON CLAY; died young.

VIII. THOMAS HELM CLAY, born October 4, 1838; married (1) Hetty M. Talbot; (2) Mrs. Mollie Collins.
IX. MARY C. CLAY, born July 2, 1840; died December 24, 1876.
X. MARTHA N. CLAY, born April 4, 1842; married Emile F. Nelson January 1, 1885.
XI. SUSANNA F. CLAY, born August 5, 1841.

85. Sally Clay married, May 25, 1780, William Buckner, son of Thomas and Elizabeth (Hawes) Buckner. Issue:

177.   I. ELIZABETH BUCKNER.
II. HENRY BUCKNER; married Susan Holt, daughter of Joseph Holt, of Bourbon County. Issue: Nellie Holt.
III. BENJAMIN BUCKNER; married Mary Spears. No issue.

86. Joseph Helm Clay, born October 22, 1803, died January 27, 1847; married, February 1, 1832, Amanda Fitz Allen Scott, daughter of Samuel Delay and Elizabeth (Cunningham) Scott, who came from the Shenandoah Valley to Kentucky, and the granddaughter of Benjamin Scott and Madame —— Delay, from Paris, France. Issue:

I. ROBERT HENRY CLAY, born December 31, 1832; killed in battle August 28, 1863.
II. MARY E. CLAY, born July 1, 1834; died July 22, 1862; married Jacob S. Megee. Issue:
I. JOSEPH CLAY MEGEE; married Lila Phillips. Issue: William H. and Harry Clay Megee.
II. MATTIE LOU MEGEE; died October 2, 1881; married George Stone, of Versailles. Issue: Clay Stone.

III. ANN REBECCA MEGEE ; resides in Paris, Kentucky.
IV. ROBERT H. MEGEE, of Jessamine County, Kentucky.

III. ANN REBECCA CLAY, born March 20, 1836; died August
16, 1854.

IV. SAMUEL SCOTT CLAY, born December 27, 1837; died March
10, 1869; married Lizzie D. Kimbrough, of Harrison
County, daughter of John M. and Susan Jones Kimbrough, and granddaughter of William and Elizabeth
(Jameson) Kimbrough, of Virginia. Issue :

I. JOHN MATT CLAY.
II. ALICE M. (BIRDIE) CLAY; married Washington
Webb.
III. SUSAN E. CLAY.
IV. ANN REBECCA CLAY.
V. HENRY SCOTT CLAY.

V. JOSEPH LARUE CLAY; died young.

VI. ISAAC C. CLAY, born March 24, 1841; married, June 2,
1870, Elizabeth A., daughter of General Thomas
Morgan and Mary Baxter Tebbs Forman, of Mason
County. Issue :

I. MARY WHITTINGTON CLAY; married Gerritt Henry
Albers, Circuit Court Commissioner of Grand
Rapids, Michigan.
II. SADIE MCDONALD CLAY; married J. William
Waterfill, of Anderson County. Issue : Robert
W. Waterfill.
III. JOSEPH SCOTT CLAY, Professor of Stenography
at Bingham School, North Carolina.
IV. SUSAN RYAN CLAY; died in infancy.

VII. SARAH MARGARET CLAY.

VIII. LETTIE L. CLAY.

IX. WILLIAM H. CLAY; died in childhood.

---

87. Henrietta Clay married (1) Frank P. Bedford.
Issue: Frank Bedford. (2) Robert Scott, who left one

child ; (3) Reverend E. S. Dudley, whose first wife was
her sister, Mary Ann Clay. Issue :

> I. NANCY DUDLEY ; married J. B. McClintock, of Harrison
> County.
> II. REBECCA DUDLEY.
> III. J. AMBROSE DUDLEY, born November 18, 1847 ; married,
> in 1865, Lizzie, daughter of W. B. Kenny, of Bourbon
> County. Issue : Eldred S. and W. K. Dudley.

---

88. Rachel Elizabeth Clay, born July 8, 1812, is yet
living, and has contributed many interesting facts to these
sketches. She married, December 23, 1830, Douglas
Payne Lewis, son of Colonel Thomas and Elizabeth Payne
Lewis. Colonel Lewis served in the Revolutionary War ;
was a member of the first Constitutional Convention of
Kentucky ; was a member of the first State Senate, and
became the fourth Judge of the Lexington Circuit. Douglas
P. Lewis was born August 4, 1804, and died October 26,
1867. Was a Representative from Bourbon in the Legislature in the forties. His sister, Sally Lewis, married
General Green Clay. Issue :

> 178. I. ELIZABETH PAYNE LEWIS.
> II. STEPHEN D. LEWIS ; married Helen Johnson. Issue :
> William and Helen Lewis.
> III. THOMAS HENRY LEWIS ; married Lucy Spears. Issue :
> Thomas S. Lewis, of Lexington.
> 179. IV. MARGARET HELM LEWIS.
> V. DOUGLAS P. LEWIS ; married ——— Johns. Issue : D. P.
> Lewis, junior.

VI. Asa K. Lewis. (See 32.)
180. VII. Mary Letitia Lewis.
VIII. Edward Alpheus Lewis.
IX. Howard Lewis.
X. Frank Clay Lewis; married Vera Rutledge, of St. Louis, Missouri.

---

89. Samuel Clay, of "Marchemont," born April 8, 1815; married, in 1836, Nancy T. Wornall, daughter of Thomas and Sally Ryan Wornall. Inheriting about four hundred acres of land from his father, he possessed, at the time of his death, February 14, 1888, many thousand valuable acres. This fortune was acquired without speculation, and was the result of indomitable energy and fine judgment, coupled with keen executive ability. His aged wife, a noble helpmeet, is still living at "Chasteney Park," Bourbon County. Issue: Five children, two of whom, Alfred and Sarah, died in childhood. Others were:

I. Thomas Henry Clay, born July 28, 1840; married, July 26, 1864, Fannie Conn, daughter of Major George W. and Winnefred (Webb) Williams, long and prominently identified with the Christian Church at Paris, Kentucky, of which Mr. Clay is a much interested officer. His residence, "The Heights," is one of the most beautiful of the far-famed Bluegrass homes, where he and Mrs. Clay dispense an elegant and generous hospitality. Issue: Roger F. (died in infancy), Alfred, George Williams, Thomas Henry, junior, and Nannine W. Clay.

II. Susan E. Clay, born September 2, 1846. (See C. M. Clay's line.)

III. JAMES E. CLAY, born September 5, 1850; married, November 15, 1871, Elizabeth, daughter of Charleton Alexander, of Paris, Kentucky. James inherited the beautiful old homestead, "Marchemont," and with it the good judgment and fine executive ability of his father, and is already extending his large estate. Issue:

    I. BELLE BRENT CLAY; married, November 15, 1893, Miller Ward, son of Judge J. Quincy and Mary E. (Miller) Ward. Issue.

    II. SAMUEL CLAY.

    III. NANNIE CLAY.

    IV. JAMES CLAY.

90. Mary Ann Clay married Reverend E. S. Dudley, of the Baptist Church, son of General James Dudley, Captain of the War of 1812. Issue:

    I. MARY E. DUDLEY; married —— Cunningham.

91. Francis Povall Clay, of "Castle Comfort," Bourbon County, married, October 27, 1842, Susan (Ryan) Wornall, daughter of Thomas and Sarah (Ryan) Wornall. Issue:

    I. WORNALL CLAY, born December 17, 1843; died October 4, 1850.

    II. WILLIAM H. CLAY; married, November 3, 1869, Emily Spears, daughter of John and Emily (Morin) Spears. Issue: John Spears, Frank Povall, William H., junior, Matthew M., Noah, and Roby Wornall Clay. Of these, only Matthew and Roby are living.

    III. HENRIETTA CLAY, born August 6, 1849; died October 4, 1850.

    VI. FRANK POVALL, JUNIOR.

    V. NANNIE CLAY; married, October 13, 1880, Walker Buckner. (See 32.) Issue: Walker B., junior, Sue Clay, Woodford, Frank P. (dead), and William Buckner.

    VI. OLIVER PERRY CLAY; married, February 9, 1892, Willie Kern. Issue: Elinor Branham Clay.

21

92. Thomas Bedford married Cordelia Thomas, of Nelson County. Issue:

    I. MARGARET.
    II. MARY.
    III. ANN.
    IV. CORDELIA.
        (These four sisters became successively the wives of Harvey Berniss, son of Reverend John Berniss, of the Presbyterian Church.)
    V. MILDRED BEDFORD; married John M. Muir, of Bardstown, Kentucky. Issue: Annie Muir.
    VI. BENJAMIN BEDFORD; died unmarried.

93. Benjamin Bedford married —— West. Issue:

    I. ARCHIBALD BEDFORD; married Martha, daughter of John Bedford, of Nelson County.
    II. BENJAMIN BEDFORD.
    III. EDWARD BEDFORD.
    IV. HILLARY BEDFORD.
    V. SALLIE BEDFORD; married Richard Milton, of Nelson County.
    VI. LETITIA BEDFORD; married Charles Milton, of Nelson County.
    VII. ELIZA BEDFORD; married Simon Snyder, of Spencer County.
    VIII. REBECCA BEDFORD; married Judge Combes, of Dallas, Texas.

94. Hillary Mosely Bedford married Miss Chadwell, of Jessamine County. Issue:

    I. RYLAND T. DILLARD BEDFORD; married Mrs. Wilson, of Franklin County.
    II. THOMAS BEDFORD; married —— Harper, of Woodford County.
    III. WILLIAM BEDFORD; married Ida Allen, of Shelby County.
    IV. HILLARY BEDFORD; married —— Harper, of Mason County.
    V. MARY ELLIS BEDFORD; died unmarried.
    VI. ANN R. BEDFORD; married Aleck Macklin.

95. Henry C. Bedford, of Bourbon County, married (1) Miss Hutchison, (2) Miss Hutchison, (3) Lucy Ware, daughter of Thompson Ware, born April 5, 1769; moved to Kentucky in 1784; married —— Conn. Thompson Ware was son of Doctor James Ware, born March 13, 1741, and his wife, Catherine Todd, who moved to Kentucky, accompanied by the Webb family, June 16, 1791. Doctor James Ware was son of James Ware, senior (born November 15, 1714), and Agnes, his wife (born December 20, 1714), of Leicester County, Virginia. H. C. Bedford had issue:

    I. WILLIAM BEDFORD.
    II. KATE BEDFORD (issue of third marriage); married Samuel S. Clay. (See 83.)

96. A. Coleman Bedford married (1) Susan Burns, (2) Mrs. Lucinda (Hedges) Wornall, (3) Mrs. Hawkins. Issue:

    I. MARY K. BEDFORD, born 1847; married Felix Lowry. Issue: Lucy and Kate Lowry.
    II. HENRY BEDFORD; married —— Dillard. Issue.
    III. WILLIAM BEDFORD.

97. Asa B. Bedford married, May 8, 1834, Davidella Ware. Issue:

    I. DOCTOR THOMPSON WARE BEDFORD; married Mildred Hutchins, of Nelson County.
    II. DOCTOR JAMES H. BEDFORD; married (1) Martha ——, (2) Mrs. Mary (Rose) Taylor. Issue:

I. Asa Bedford; died young.
II. Doctor Charles Bedford, of Owensboro.
III. Mary F. (Bedford) Brown.
IV. Lucy (Bedford) Mattingly, of Daviess County, Kentucky.

---

98. Mary Clay Bedford married N. G. Thomas, of Nelson County.   Issue :

             I. A. C. Thomas; married Lizzie Cox. Issue.
181.   II. Margaret Thomas; married Doctor Isaac McCloskey.
182.   III. Henry Clay Thomas, born August, 1833.
             IV. Doctor James G. Thomas; married Margaret Owens, of Savannah, Georgia. Issue.
             V. S. M. Thomas, of Mississippi, married Josephine Davenport. Issue.
             VI. Mary Clay Thomas; married (1) Samuel McBride, of Boyle County; (2) Alexander McMeekin, of Nelson County. Issue : Mary, Samuel, and Archie McBride.

---

99. Charles Clay Black married Jane Allin Roch. Issue. William, Mary, Martha, George W., and Letitia Black died young.   Those surviving :

             I. Elizabeth Black; married John Macklin. Issue :
                I. Emma Macklin; married Burbridge Blackburn.
                II. Anna Macklin; married Reverend Thomas J. Stevenson. Issue : John Macklin and Mary Emma Stevenson.
             II. Stephen Black; married Lydia Macklin. Issue : Howard Black; married Mary Westfall. Issue : Stephen and Charles Westfall Black.
             III. Sarah Allin Black; married Charles C. Lecompte. Issue : Charles Black (died 1889), Joseph, and Margaret Lecompte.

100. Stephen Black married Patsy Williams in 1819. Issue all died young except:

  I. SAMUEL BLACK, who married, December, 1848, Mary Williamson, granddaughter of Absolem Chenowith, of Jefferson County. Issue:
    I. STEPHEN BLACK; married Hallie Cox. No issue.
    II. FRANKLIN P. BLACK; died unmarried.
    III. CHARLES BLACK. Issue: Mary Lillian Black.
    IV. JOHN E. BLACK. Issue: John Edward Black.
    V. MARTHA BLACK; married J. H., son of Charles Tucker. Issue: Linna Bell.
    VI. WILLIAM DENTON; died in infancy.

---

101. Elizabeth Black married Balzar Mantle. Issue:

  I. MARY MANTLE; married Colonel Fichey. No issue.
  II. ELIZABETH MANTLE; married Sterling Hubbard. Issue:
    I. DOCTOR WILLIAM STERLING, of New York.
    II. CHARLES M. HUBBARD.
    III. HARRY F. HUBBARD.
    IV. KATE HUBBARD; married S. D. Chaseldine.
    V. MARGARET HUBBARD.
    VI. JENNIE HUBBARD; married Xerxes Farrar, of Ohio.
    VII. IDA HUBBARD; married Walter Whittlesey, of Chelsea, Massachusetts.
  III. NARCISSUS MANTLE; married Horace Putman. Issue: Charles, William, Horace, and Elizabeth, who married Doctor Quinn.
  IV. SUSAN MANTLE; married Edward Hill. Issue: John Hill.
  V. CHARLES H. MANTLE: married (1) Jennie Mooney; (2) Henrietta Miller, daughter of Doctor Henry Miller, of Louisville, who left:
    I. CLARA MANTLE; married J. W. Biles, of Cincinnati.
    II. BESSIE MANTLE.
    III. CHARLES MANTLE.
        Charles H. Mantle married (3) Emma Brown. Issue:
    IV. EMMA MANTLE.
    V. MARY MANTLE.
    VI. BROWN MANTLE.
        Charles H. Mantle died March 11, 1899.

102. Harriet Elizabeth Fort, born December 23, 1822 ; married, December 2, 1841, E. D. Smith.   Issue :

    I. GANSVOORT SMITH ; died young.
    II. HILLIARD SMITH.
    III. POLONA SMITH, born February 13, 1848 ; married and has issue.
    IV. JOSIAH FORT SMITH ; died in infancy.

103. Susan Green Fort, born September 3, 1824; married, December 8, 1842, Robert J. Battle.   Issue :

    I. SUSAN BATTLE : married (1) Reverend —— Newton ; (2) Reverend —— Long.
    II. SARAH BATTLE ; married William Burton.
    III. JOSIAH BATTLE ; married Lou Nelse.
    IV. MARY BATTLE.
    V. HATTIE BATTLE ; married Professor Terrill.
    VI. IDA BATTLE ; married Mr. Turner.

104. William Warder Fort, born March 18, 1826 ; married, September 2, 1847, Mary Ligon, and died October 25, 1852.   Issue :

    I. CORNELIA FORT ; married William Campbell.   Issue : Cornelia Campbell, of Galveston, Texas.
    II. JOSIAH FORT ; died in infancy.

105. Doctor Joseph Marston Fort married (1), November 6, 1849, Jack Anne Fort, born December 8, 1829, died July 20, 1882 ; went to Texas in 1850.   Issue: Eliz-

abeth Lawson, Diana Coleman, John Digges, Diana Coleman (2), William Lawson, and Harriet Eugenia Fort died young. The others were:

    I. MIRIAM ROBERT FORT, born August 22, 1861; married, November 6, 1879, William Francis Gill, son of William H. Gill, of Maryland. Issue:
        I. JOSEPH HENRY GILL, born September 15, 1886.
        II. MURRAY FRANCIS GILL, born October 4, 1888.
    II. JOSEPHA MARSTON FORT, born November 5, 1865; married, November 5, 1885, Thadeus Stocks Preston, son of John Preston, of Georgia. Issue: Miriam Fort and Cornelia Preston.
        Doctor J. M. Fort married (2) November 1, 1883, Mrs. Mary Dancy Fort. Issue:
    III. WILLIAM FELTS FORT, born November 7, 1887.

---

106. Frances Wilson Lockett married in 1815 Doctor Philip Turner Southall, of Prince Edward County, Virginia. He was son of Major Stephen Southall, of the Revolution, and Martha Wood, and grandson of Colonel Turner Southall and Martha Vandewall. Martha Wood was the daughter of Colonel Valentine Wood and Lucy Henry, daughter of Colonel John Henry, the immigrant from Scotland, and sister of Governor Patrick Henry, of Virginia. Issue:

183.   I. STEPHEN OSBORNE SOUTHALL.
184.   II. PHILIP FRANCIS SOUTHALL, M. D.

107. Martha A. Trabue married George T. Thompson. Issue :

      I. AGNES W. THOMPSON ; married George G. A. Bryan. Issue : Agnes T. Bryan.

      II. BESSIE THOMPSON ; married John P. W. Brown. Issue : George T., Ella P., John P. W., junior, and Samuel P. Brown.

      III. CHARLES T. THOMPSON ; married Elizabeth Weeks. Issue : Hill T., Fannie T., George A. B. T., and Allan W. Thompson.

      IV. MATTIE W. THOMPSON.

      V. FANNIE THOMPSON.

      VI. J. HILL THOMPSON ; married Agnes M. Ricketts.

      VII. JANE R. THOMPSON ; married Alfred E. Howell. Issue : Morton B., Martha, and Frances Howell.

      VIII. KATE THOMPSON ; married Joseph L. Weakley. Issue : Martha Weakley.

---

108. Anthony F. Trabue married Christine Manly. Issue :

      I. MARTHA T. TRABUE ; married Bragg Glasscock. Issue : Ethel Glenn and Laura Glasscock.

      II. CHRISTINE TRABUE ; married W. G. Robertson. Issue : Kitty, Christine, and William G. Robertson.

      III. TAYLOR JONES TRABUE ; married Honour Williamson. Issue : Van Culin Trabue.

      IV. MARY GLENN TRABUE ; married Samuel D. Shaw.

---

109. Jane W. Trabue married John H. Reynolds. Issue :

      I. CHARLES T. REYNOLDS ; married Jennie Peyton.

      II. JOHN H. REYNOLDS ; married Lollie Smith. Issue : William H. and John H. Reynolds.

      III. ALICE A. REYNOLDS.

      IV. MARTHA T. REYNOLDS ; married John Adger. Issue : Jane T. Adger.

V. Anthony T. Reynolds.
VI. George F. Reynolds; married Mary Bruner. Issue:
Mary Reynolds.

---

110. Sarah E. Trabue married (1) John B. Stevens,
(2) William R. Stivers. Issue:

I. Johnnette B. Stevens; married Cyrus S. Steere. Issue:
Sallie T., Albert C., Mable G., Nellie L., Grace,
Johnnette C., and Cyrus S. Steere, junior.

---

111. Charles C. Trabue, a Southern soldier, was mortally wounded and buried on the battlefield at Sharpsburg,
Maryland, September 19, 1862.

---

112. Robert W. Trabue married Mary Bibb. Issue:

I. Joan Trabue; married William Winn. Issue: Nellie and
Robert T. Winn.
II. Addie Trabue; married George Briscoe. Issue: Owen
Trabue Briscoe.
III. Christine Trabue.

---

113. Jane E. Russell, born July 30, 1794; died January 10, 1861; married, October 16, 1816, Reverend
Claiborne Duval, a Methodist minister. Issue:

I. John Claiborne Duval; died young.
II. Anne E. Duval; married (1) John Gale; (2) James W. C.
Houston, of Union County, Kentucky. Issue: Claiborne
Henry Gale and John A. Gale.
III. Doctor W. C. Duval, of Pineville, Missouri; married (1)
P. E. Holland; (2) Sarah F. Pearson; (3) Mary Jane
Boyer; (4) Thursa T. Wood. Issue:

22

I. ANNE E. DUVAL; died in infancy.

II. NEY DUVAL, born May 4, 1854; died November 7, 1873.

III. ELDORA DUVAL, born October 24, 1855; married, December 19, 1873, J. M. Warmack. Issue: William E., Matthew P., Jesse N., and Elizabeth E. Warmack.

IV. CLAIBORNE E. DUVAL, born December 25, 1858; married, February 23, 1882, Mary Jane Hamilton. Issue: Clarice Duval.

V. ALICE DUVAL; died in infancy,

VI. SARAH FRANCES DUVAL, born March 26, 1866; married, September 5, 1883, Doctor S. D. Preston, of Missouri.

VII. ANNE ELIZA DUVAL, born September 20, 1867.

VIII. ROSE DUVAL; died in infancy.

IX. MARY JANE DUVAL, born July 9, 1881.

X. WILLIAM CLAUDE DUVAL; died in infancy.

XI. CLARENCE DUVAL, born May 9, 1883.

XII. CYNTHIA L. DUVAL, born May 17, 1884.

IV. JOHN W. DUVAL; died unmarried in 1851.

V. ELEAZER DUVAL; died young.

VI. CAROLINE T. DUVAL; married John Ewell. Issue: John Gale, Emma R., Anna M., Cynthia E., Lena H., Carrie B., Claude D., Edwin E., and Clara Louise Ewell.

VII. HARDY M. C. DUVAL; married Eliza Mobley. Issue:

I. CLAUDE H. DUVAL, of Illinois. Issue: Carrie G. Duval.

II. LAVINIA J. DUVAL; married Louie Meyer. Issue: Duval and Maggie Meyer.

III. FANNIE BELL DUVAL; married David Brenneke, of Indiana.

IV. DORA HOUSTON DUVAL.

V. MAGGIE T. DUVAL.

VI. MANNIE M. DUVAL.

VII. WILLIAM J. DUVAL.

VIII. CLAIBORNE M. DUVAL.

IX. GALE B. DUVAL (dead).

X. KATE HARRIS DUVAL.

114. Tabitha Adams Russell married, August 1, 1818, Lucius C. Duval, of Union County. Issue :

I. JOHN RUSSELL DUVAL, died in 1879; married and had issue :
    I. ROBERT DUVAL, of Monticello, Arkansas.
    II. MARTHA DUVAL ; married —— Ashe, of Texas.
    III. ELIZABETH DUVAL ; married —— Symmes.
II. MARY ANNE DUVAL, born January 28, 1821 ; married Mr. Rowley, of Union County, Kentucky. Issue :
    I. ROBERT ROWLEY; married Lucy Hodge, of Louisville. Issue : Kenneth.
    II. JAMES ROWLEY, of Union County ; married Julia Hodge. Issue : Cora.
    III. WILLIAM ROWLEY, of New York City.
    IV. LEE ROWLEY ; unmarried.
III. ELIZA P. DUVAL ; died young.
IV. LUCIUS C. DUVAL ; died young.
V. MARTHA L. DUVAL ; died young.
VI. WILLIAM H. C. DUVAL, born November 8, 1829, is unmarried, and lives in California.
VII. TABITHA ADAMS DUVAL, born June 21, 1831 ; married John R. D. Byrne, of Hopkins County, Kentucky. Issue :
    I. JOHN BYRNE ; married Hannah Sisk. Issue : Katie, Lucius, and Robert Byrne.
    II. SARAH BYRNE ; married John Bruce, of Hopkins County. Issue : Charles and Walter Bruce.
    III. CHARLES BYRNE ; unmarried.
VIII. SAMUEL C. DUVAL, born March 8, 1834 ; lives at Alexandria, Texas ; married Mrs. M. A. Short April 10, 1879. Issue : Pearl, Cordelia, and Henry Edward Duval.
IX. CHARLES T. DUVAL, born May 22, 1836, of California ; married Malinda J. Bruton. Issue : Annie and Lucius Duval.
X. EDWARD R. DUVAL ; died young.
XI. DANIEL A. DUVAL, born March 22, 1841 ; died at Fredericksburg, Virginia, September 26, 1861.

115. Lavinia Green Russell died in 1874; married Doctor William B. Dozier, of Mississippi.   Issue:

> I. DOCTOR A. McLEAN DOZIER; married Mary R. Pool. Issue: Lavinia E., Malvina A., Mary, John D., Charlotte L., William A., Celester C., and Elijah Pool Dozier.

---

116. Doctor William Clay Russell, of Elkton, Kentucky, married, in 1857, Mary S. Farley, of Virginia. Issue:

> I. HATTIE E. RUSSELL; married O. A. McLeod. Issue: William and Russell McLeod.
> II. MARY A. RUSSELL.
> III. JOHN W. RUSSELL.
> IV. JAMES DANIEL RUSSELL.
> V. CORINNE E. RUSSELL.
> VI. CLAUDE C. RUSSELL.

---

117. Thomas Clay McCreery, born 1816; died in 1890. In 1845 he married Clara Hawes, and settled at Owensboro, Kentucky.   Issue:

> I. SAMUEL McCREERY, born 1845; died in 1851.
> II. ROBERT McCREERY, born 1847; died 1876; married Cleline Athey. Issue: Robert Athey; married Wynn Dixon, and has one child, Cleline A. Dickson.
> III. DECIUS McCREERY, born 1850; died 1866.
> IV. SALLIE McCREERY, born 1851; married John W. Matthews. Issue: Clara, Lucy Clay, and Elizabeth Matthews.
> V. CLARA E. McCREERY, born 1853; died 1880; married Lee Lumpkin. Issue: Clara Lee Lumpkin.
> VI. CYNTHIA GREEN CLAY McCREERY, born 1855; married W. A. Stuart. Issue: Nellie, Robert, James, and Kitty Stuart.

"Few men ever occupied a seat in the United States Senate who looked so thoroughly a Senator as did Thomas Clay McCreery, who represented Kentucky in that body. His figure was full and his presence imposing. His large, well-shaped head was well set between massive shoulders. His face was broad, his eyes keen and expressive, his mouth wide, his lips well-shaped, and his forehead majestic. He always wore a dress coat, and moved heavily, as if his bulky body contained a burden of thought heavier than the flesh.

"Looking down from the gallery now, one can find no figure so suggestive of the dignity and beauty of the office, no face whose strong outlines so strikingly reveals the profound and thoughtful expression of Webster. He loved the seclusion of his own home and the treasures of his own library. No one ever questioned the honor or purity of his character or the charms of his accomplishments. His voracious reading had enriched a mind naturally receptive and brilliant, and his own style of composition was modelled after the finest specimens of the English classics."

Senator McCreery was born in Kentucky in 1817, and was a student at Centre College, Danville. Studied law, but turned his attention to agriculture. Was a candidate for Presidential Elector in 1852; was defeated, but in 1860 was elected, and voted for Breckenridge and Lane; was United States Senator from 1868 to 1879. Died in 1890.

_____

118. Sally Anne Lewis Clay Smith, born July 10, 1818; married, December 3, 1835, David Short Goodloe, born November 3, 1811, whose father, William Goodloe, was born in 1769 in Northampton County, North Carolina, and came to Kentucky in 1787, at the age of eighteen years, and settled on Otter Creek, Madison County, three miles east of Richmond. In 1796 he married Susan Woods, daughter of Captain Archival Woods, of Revolutionary fame. David Short Goodloe was born and reared in Madison County, but removed, with his family, to Lexington in 1845; was elected Major-General of the State Militia in 1851, and thus acquired the title by which he was thereafter known. He was an "Old-line Whig" and bitterly opposed to Secession. He held several positions of trust under the National Government; was United States Assessor under President Lincoln, and served as Revenue Agent and Supervisor of Internal Revenue for nearly the entire South and West, and later United States Pension Agent; was a devoted Mason, and attained the second highest position within the gift of the Order in the United States.

Mrs. Goodloe was a fine character, possessing a strong, well-cultured mind, and, though decided and unswerving in her convictions, was regarded with love and admiration by her family and friends. She died September 25, 1875, as she had lived, a true and faithful Christian. To General and Mrs. Goodloe were born:

185.
    I. SPEED SMITH GOODLOE.
    II. DAVID S. GOODLOE, a physician of Lexington.
186.
    III. WILLIAM CASSIUS GOODLOE, born June 27, 1841.
    IV. GREEN CLAY GOODLOE is Paymaster of the Navy, a life position which he has ably and honorably filled for many years. He married Bettie, daughter of Honorable James B. Beck, for several terms United States Senator from Kentucky, a man loved and honored of all men. Major and Mrs. Goodloe have no children.

119. Doctor Curran Smith, of Richmond, Kentucky, is a man universally beloved for his many virtues and generous qualities. He married, in 1854, Sallie W. Goodloe, daughter of Judge William E. Goodloe, of Lexington. Issue:

    I. MARY SPEED SMITH.
    II. ALMA GOODLOE SMITH; married Reverend H. M. Rogers, and resides at Dayton, Indiana. Issue: Bessie, Goodloe, Louise Tinsley, Mary Spencer, and James Speed Rogers.
    III. JOHN SPEED SMITH, of Washington, D. C.
    IV. BESSIE SMITH; married James Benton, a lawyer of Winchester, Kentucky. Issue: Curran and Sarah Goodloe Benton.
    V. CURRALEEN SMITH.
    VI. WILLIE C. SMITH (twin with Curraleen).

120. General Green Clay Smith, born July 2, 1832, had a distinguished career. At fifteen years of age he volunteered for the Mexican War. Was elected Second Lieutenant of Captain James Stone's Company in Colonel Humphrey Marshall's Regiment of Cavalry. He studied law, and practiced in Richmond and Covington; served in the Kentucky Legislature in 1860; during the Civil War entered the Union Army and became Colonel of the Fourth Kentucky Cavalry; commanded that regiment until 1862, when he was made Brigadier General and appointed to a Brigade of Cavalry in General Rosecrans' Army; was brevetted Major General in 1863 for gallant services; elected to Congress in 1863; appointed Governor of Montana; in 1876 was Presidential candidate on the Prohibition ticket, and finally gave up politics and became a minister in the Baptist Church. He possessed talents of a high order, and for nine years was Moderator of General Association of Kentucky Baptists; was pastor of the Richmond and the Mount Sterling churches, and of the Metropolitan Church of Washington, D. C. He married Lena Duke, daughter of James H. Duke, of Scott County. She was a grand-niece of Chief Justice Marshall. Issue:

    I. ELIZA CLAY SMITH; married James B. Hawkins, and died in 1891.
    II. MARY BUFORD SMITH.
    III. KEITH DUKE SMITH.
    IV. LENA DUKE SMITH; married John Whitehead.
    V. GREEN CLAY SMITH.

Honorable HORATIO W. BRUCE.   Honorable THOMAS C. McCREARY

121. Pauline Smith, born September 30, 1829, married Guilford A. Talbott, of Boyle County, Kentucky. Issue :

    I. THOMAS JACKSON TALBOTT.
    II. MARIA E. TALBOTT ; married Charles Dunn.
    III. MARY J. TALBOTT.
    IV. HENRY TALBOTT.
    V. ALBERT TALBOTT.
    VI. PAULINE TALBOTT.

---

122. Eliza Rodes and Robert Stone, of Texas, had issue :

    I. SALLIE STONE ; married John Edwards. Issue : Sallie and Robert Stone Edwards, of Cottleville, Missouri.
    II. RODES STONE.
    III. JAMES STONE.
    IV. KATE STONE ; married John Edwards.
    V. ROBERT H. STONE, JUNIOR.
    VI. CALEB S. STONE.
    VII. PAULINE STONE.

---

123. Sallie Rodes married John Watson, of Frankfort, and had issue :

    I. PAULINE CLAY WATSON ; married Reverend Robert Christie, and had Robert and Mary Rodes Christie, of Pittsburgh.
    II. WILLIAM RODES WATSON.
    III. HENRY HOWE WATSON.
    IV. ADALINE CRITTENDEN WATSON ; married Knox Brown. Issue : John Watson and Knox Brown, junior.
    V. ELIZA WATSON ; married William McCuen. Issue : Sallie Rodes and William McCuen.
    VI. DUDLEY WATSON.

124. Martha Green Rodes married Reverend Robert
Breck, D. D., born in Richmond, Kentucky, May 8,
1827; graduated from Centre College at the age of sev-
enteen, and later from the Theological Seminary of
Princeton College, New Jersey, which institution has
since conferred on him the degree of Doctor of Divinity.
He was the son of Judge Daniel Breck, a member of
Congress and a Judge of the Court of Appeals of Kentucky.   They had issue :

    I. PAULINE RODES BRECK.
    II. JANE TODD BRECK ; married Hugh Anderson Moran.
    III. WILLIAM RODES BRECK.
    IV. SALLY WATSON BRECK ; married Lucas Brodhead.
    V. DANIEL BRECK, born at Richmond, Kentucky, July 27,
        1861 ; graduated from Central University, and later
        took a post-graduate course in the California Uni-
        versity.   He has been a successful civil engineer, and
        is at present in the office of the President of the
        Louisville & Nashville Railroad, at Louisville.
    VI. BELLE McDOWELL BRECK.

---

125. Belle Rodes and John Harvie McDowell, of Cincinnati, Ohio, had issue :

    I. JOSEPH J. McDOWELL.
    II. WILLIAM RODES McDOWELL.
    III. JOHN HARVIE McDOWELL, JUNIOR.
    IV. MARTHA RODES McDOWELL ; married Doctor Frank M.
        Hanger, of Staunton, Virginia.   Issue : Franklin McC.
        and William Rodes McD. Hanger.
    V. BELLE RODES McDOWELL.

126. Martha Clay, whom the writer remembers as a well-poised, interesting woman, was born February 1, 1832, and married Henry B. Davenport, of Virginia, January 5, 1860. Issue:

    I. JUNIUS B. DAVENPORT, born October 3, 1860.
    II. EZEKIEL FIELD DAVENPORT, born January 9, 1864.
    III. HENRY B. DAVENPORT, born February 11, 1865.
    IV. AMELIA CLAY DAVENPORT; married Catesby Woodford.
    V. BRAXTON DAVENPORT.

127. Christopher F. Clay, born in Bourbon County November 20, 1835; married, June, 1867, Mary F. Brooks, daughter of Samuel Brooks, of Bourbon County. Issue:

    I. BRUTUS J. CLAY, born 1868.
    II. SAMUEL BROOKS CLAY, born 1876.
    III. NANNIE WOODFORD CLAY, born 1874.
    IV. SADIE BROOKS CLAY, born 1876.
    V. CHRISTOPHER FIELD CLAY.
    VI. MARTHA DAVENPORT CLAY, born 1879.

128. Green Clay, born in Bourbon County February 11, 1839; married, in 1871, Jane Rhodes, of New Orleans. After graduating from Yale College and Cambridge Law School, he was abroad for eight years—one year as Secretary to Honorable C. M. Clay, United States Minister to Russia, and seven years as Secretary of Legation to Minister Marsh in Italy. On his return home he became a cotton-planter. Is now a resident of Missouri. Issue:

    I. GREEN CLAY, JUNIOR, born in 1872; married Louise Campbell in 1896, and died three months thereafter.
    II. RODES CLAY, born 1874.
    III. CASSIUS M. CLAY (III), born in 1879.
    IV. JANIE C. CLAY, born 1886.

129. Ezekiel Field Clay was born in Bourbon County December 1, 1840, and resides at "Runnymede," his beautiful country-seat, in the midst of happiness and prosperity. He married, May 8, 1866, Mary L., the accomplished daughter of John T. Woodford and his wife, Elizabeth Buckner, the granddaughter of Colonel Henry Clay, of Bourbon County.

Colonel E. F. Clay was a student at Kentucky University when war was declared in 1861, and at once enlisted in the First Kentucky Mounted Riflemen, Confederate States Army, as a private. Later he organized a company, of which he was chosen Captain, with William Talbott, Harry Clay, and James T. Rogers, of "New Forest," as Lieutenants. Afterward was promoted Lieutenant - Colonel, and commanded his regiment until the close of the war. Colonel Clay was seriously wounded and taken prisoner at Puncheon Creek, Magoffin County, and remained at Johnson's Island for nine months. He was a brave and gallant soldier. His regiment was a part of General Humphrey Marshall's Command, Department of Southwestern Virginia and Eastern Kentucky. Issue :

     I. Ezekiel Field Clay, junior, born June 16, 1871 ; married Anna C., daughter of Judge J. Quincey and Mary E. (Miller) Ward, of "Sunny Side."

    II. Woodford Clay, born July 17, 1873.

   III. Brutus J. Clay, born November 27, 1875.

   IV. Buckner Clay, born December 30, 1877.

    V. Amelia Field Clay, born February 15, 1880.

   VI. Mary Catesby Clay, born June 17, 1883.

130. Cassius M. Clay, junior, of Bourbon County, was born March 26, 1846. Inherited and resides at "Auvergne," the beautiful old home of his father. Mr. Clay is a prominent citizen and politician of Bourbon County, having served as State Senator and in the last Constitutional Convention of Kentucky. Has been three times married : (1) January 27, 1869, to Susan E. Clay, daughter of Samuel and Susan (Wornall) Clay ; (2) November 29, 1882, to Pattie T. Lyman ; (3) December 6, 1888, to Mary Blythe Harris, daughter of Honorable John D. Harris, of Richmond, Kentucky, who descends through William Harris, John Harris, and Christopher Harris from Major Robert Harris, a member of the House of Burgesses of Virginia. Mr. Clay had issue by his first wife :

  I. JUNIUS BRUTUS CLAY, born April 25, 1871.
  II. SAMUEL HENRY CLAY, born April 7, 1873; died December 9, 1895.
  III. ANNIE LOUISE CLAY, born September 22, 1877.
  IV. SUSAN ELIZABETH CLAY, born April 3, 1880.
   (Mr. Clay had by his second wife a daughter, who died in infancy. In his present marriage there have been born :)
  VI. INFANT DAUGHTER, born and died September 29, 1893.
  VII. CASSIUS M. CLAY (IV), born March 2, 1895.
  VIII. JOHN HARRIS CLAY, born March 27, 1897.

---

131. Green Clay, born in Madison County in 1837, died June 21, 1883, was a Major in the volunteer service of the Civil War. He married Cornelia, daughter of Doctor Charles and Nancy Embry Walker. No issue.

132. Mary Barr Clay married Major J. Frank Herrick, of Cleveland, Ohio. Issue :

    I. CLAY HERRICK, of Hudson, Ohio.
    II. FRANK W. H. CLAY, of Washington, D. C.
    III. .GREEN CLAY, of Cincinnati.

---

133. Sarah Lewis Clay married James Bennett, of Madison County, Kentucky. Issue :

    I. MARY WARFIELD BENNETT.
    II. ELIZABETH BENNETT; married, February 2, 1898, T. J. Smith, junior.
    III. HELEN BENNETT.
    IV. LAURA CLAY BENNETT.

Mrs. Bennett and her sister, Mrs. Mary B. Clay, were the pioneer workers in the Woman's Suffrage Association of Kentucky, and its successful establishment indicates effective and intelligent labor.

---

134. Brutus Junius Clay was born in Madison County, February 20, 1847, in the same room in which his father, General Cassius M. Clay, was born, October 19, 1810, and in which the old hero still sleeps.

Mr. Clay married (1) Pattie Amelia, daughter of Colonel Christopher Irvine and Charlotte Elizabeth (Martin) Field, and granddaughter of John L. Martin, of Louisville, Kentucky. Pattie A. Field was born November 22, 1848, and died at "Linwood," Madison County, December 23, 1891. Issue :

I. BELLE LYMAN CLAY, born November 4, 1872.
II. CHRISTOPHER FIELD CLAY, born December 19, 1874.
III. ORVILLE MARTIN CLAY, born May 7, 1879.
IV. MARY WARFIELD CLAY, born September 26, 1882.
V. CHARLOTTE ELIZABETH CLAY, born May 31, 1889.

In memory of his wife Mr. Clay gave to the Pattie
A. Clay Infirmary Association, of Richmond, Kentucky, a
handsome two-story building with large and ample grounds,
in which the sick and suffering of the city may find lodg-
ment and care. A beautiful memorial to a lovely woman.

Mr. Clay married a second time to Mrs. Lalla Rookh
Marsteller, nee Fish, daughter of T. Spencer and Nannie
(Poore) Fish, of prominent New York and Massachusetts
families. Mr. Clay's education was begun under those
famous old teachers of the Bluegrass region, Abraham
Drake and B. B. Sayre, and finished at the Literary and
Civil Engineer Departments of Michigan University.
While taking an active interest in politics as a Repub-
lican, he has never held office. Was tendered the position
of United States Minister to Argentine by President
McKinley, but declined.

---

135. Laura Clay, of Lexington, Kentucky, is one
woman of the name who deserves, at the pen of the
historian, more than a passing notice, because her work
has been for others. As the acknowledged leader of the
"Woman's Suffrage" movement in Kentucky she has won

golden opinions from all. Strong in her convictions and brave in their advocacy, she impresses her hearers with the fact that she is battling for principle, not opinion, and that the work for and in behalf of that principle must be well done. To this force there is added that refined, gentle, honest bearing which has made successful her efforts as a public speaker. We wish there were more women like her.

136. Thomas H. Clay, of "Mansfield," Fayette County, Kentucky, was born September 22, 1803. He and his elder brother, Theodore W. Clay, were instructed by Amos Kendall during part of the time Henry Clay was abroad engaged in the Treaty of Ghent.

He studied law with Chief Justice Boyle; was admitted to the bar and practiced for a time at Natchez, then at Terre Haute, but finally returned to Lexington, where he and his father became much interested in the manufacture of hemp. October 5, 1837, he married Marie Mentelle, daughter of Waldemar and Charlotte LeClerc Mentelle, French emigrés from Paris, France, who left that country during the reign of terror and settled in Gallipolis. The Mentelle family later moved to Lexington, and spent their remaining days at "Rose Cottage," opposite Ashland.

Thomas H. Clay was a consistent Whig until the disruption of that party. In 1860, while a member of the legislature, he strongly opposed every endeavor to take Kentucky out of the Union. In October, 1862, Mr. Lincoln appointed him Minister Resident of the United States to the Republic of Nicaragua, where he was transferred to Honduras in 1863. His health becoming impaired, he returned to Lexington, where he died March 18, 1871. He was a man of quiet tastes, warm-hearted, a loving husband and father, and a staunch and self-sacrificing friend. Issue:

        I. LUCRETIA HART CLAY, born 1838; married W. P. C. Breck-inridge, and died at the birth of her first child, who did not long survive her.

187.   II. HARRY BOYLE CLAY.

188.   III. THOMAS HART CLAY.

        IV. ROSE VICTOIRE CLAY; married Garland Hale. No issue.

        V. MARY RUSSELL CLAY (Miss Minnie), a most interesting woman.

---

137. Ann Brown Clay, born at "Ashland," April 15, 1807; married, October 21, 1823, James Erwin, and died in 1835, leaving issue:

        I. JULIA D. ERWIN.

        II. HENRY CLAY ERWIN; married Margaret Johnson. Issue, since dead.

        III. JAMES ERWIN; died in early manhood, unmarried.

        IV. LUCRETIA HART ERWIN.

        V. ANDREW EUGENE ERWIN; married, in 1853, Josephine Russell. He was a Colonel in the Confederate Army, commanding the Sixth Missouri Regiment, and fell at the siege of Vicksburg in 1864. Issue:

I. LUCRETIA CLAY ERWIN, born June 12, 1854; married, February 5, 1876, Minor Simpson, of Fayette County. Issue: John M. Clay, Josephine Clay, Eugene Erwin, and Henry Clay Simpson.

II. NETTIE RUSSELL ERWIN, born April 20, 1857; married Howard Gratz in 1887, and died January 7, 1889, without issue.

III. MARY WEBSTER ERWIN, born February 5, 1861; married M.W. Anderson in 1890. Issue: Henry Clay, George, and Matthew W. Anderson.

IV. EUGENIA ERWIN, born January 23, 1864; died 1864.

---

138. Henry Clay, junior, was born at Lexington in 1811, and married, October 10, 1832, Julia, daughter of Thomas Prather, of Louisville. Julia Prather was born May 16, 1814, and died February 13, 1840. Thomas Prather, who died February 3, 1823, aged fifty-two years, married, February 12, 1800, Matilda Fontaine, born September 18, 1782, died Thanksgiving Day, 1850, daughter of Captain Aaron Fontaine, born in Charles City County, Virginia, November 30, 1753, and died in Louisville, April, 1823. The latter married, in 1773, Barbara Terrell, daughter of Richmond and Ann Overton Terrell, of Louisa County, Virginia. Captain Fontaine was the son of Reverend Peter Fontaine, of Westover Parish, Virginia, son of Reverend James Fontaine, a Huguenot, who in 1686 fled from France to England at the revocation of the Edict of Nantes.

Henry Clay was graduated from West Point, but resigned from the army after serving one year. He studied law, and was practicing with John I. Jacob, in Louisville, when the war with Mexico was declared. He offered his services to the State, and was appointed Lieutenant Colonel of the Second Kentucky Regiment, and was killed while gallantly leading his men at the battle of Buena Vista, February 22, 1847. Issue:

I. HENRY CLAY, born July 20, 1833, and died June 5, 1862, at Louisville, of typhoid fever, while a soldier in the Union Army.

II. MATILDA CLAY, born January 30, 1835; died at Bordeaux, France.

III. MARTHA CLAY; died in infancy.

189. IV. ANNE CLAY, born February 14, 1837.

V. THOMAS JULIAN CLAY, born January 30, 1840; died October 12, 1863, at Atlanta, Georgia, of typhoid fever, while serving as a soldier in the Confederate Army.

---

139. James Brown Clay was born November 9, 1817. In 1843 he married Susanna Maria Jacob, a daughter of John I. Jacob, of Louisville, and his wife, Lucy Donald Robertson. James B. Clay was a lawyer, and practiced with his father at the Lexington bar. In 1849 he was appointed by President Taylor United States Charge d'Affaires at Lisbon, Portugal, where he resided with his family until 1850. In 1851 he removed to St. Louis, Missouri, but afterward returned to Kentucky, and, on the death of his father, purchased Ashland and made that historic place his home. In 1856 he was

tendered by President Buchanan the Mission to Berlin, Germany, which he declined.   In 1857 he was a member of the United States House of Representatives, and declined the nomination for a second term.   In 1861 he was a member of the Peace Convention which met at Washington with a view to prevent war then threatened and impending between the North and South.   During the war his sympathies were strongly with the South, although he took no active part in the events that transpired.   He was once arrested by the Kentucky Home Guards and taken to Louisville, where, after a short detention, he was released.   To avoid further molestation he passed within the Southern lines, and when General Bragg's army evacuated Kentucky, after the battle of Perryville, he went South with it.   Soon after, hopelessly ill with consumption, he ran the blockade of the Southern coast and reached Canada, where he was joined by his family and remained until his death, which occurred January 26, 1864.   Issue :

190.   I. James Brown Clay.
         II. John C. J. Clay ; died in 1872.
191.   III. Henry Clay ; died in 1884.
192.   IV. Thomas Jacob Clay.
193.   V. Charles Donald Clay.
         VI. George Hudson Clay.
         VII. Nathaniel Hart Clay ; died young.
         VIII. Lucy Jacob Clay ; died young.
         IX. Susan Jacob Clay ; died young.
194.   X. Lucretia Hart Clay.

140. Emma Cynthia Nelson married, December 15, 1857, John Baylis Earle, born September 17, 1833; died January 30, 1869. Issue:

> I. ALLISON NELSON EARLE, born March 14, 1860; married, April 27, 1892, Annie Bocock Hix, born February 19, 1869. Issue: William Hix, Allison Nelson, Emma Cynthia, and Frances Elizabeth Earle.
> II. ANNIE ELIZA EARLE, born April 5, 1863; married, April 23, 1890, Paterich M. Farrell, born February 17, 1855. Issue: Emma Nelson, Mary, and Baylis Earle Farrell.
> III. JOHN BAYLIS EARLE, born June 20, 1866.
> IV. HENRY SEARS EARLE, born February 22, 1869; married Mattie Rogers, born August 6, 1872, died April 7, 1892. Issue: Charles Rogers Sears, died in infancy.

141. Alice Sophia Nelson married, June 8, 1865, John H. Harrison. Issue:

> I. MARY EVANS HARRISON, born July 9, 1866; married, November 26, 1885, Daniel Stonewall Eddins. Issue: Daniel Stonewall, junior, Alice, and George Morse Eddins.
> II. ALLISON NELSON HARRISON, born September 19, 1869; married, February 22, 1898, Irene Dunklin.
> III. JOHN H. HARRISON, JUNIOR, born April 1, 1872; married, April 21, 1898, Addie Earle.
> IV. JAMES E. HARRISON, born October 6, 1874; died January 3, 1877.
> V. GUY BROWN HARRISON, born November 10, 1876; married, February 12, 1898, Nora Wimple.

142. John Alston Nelson married, January 1, 1871, Georgia Alice Little. Issue:

I. Mary Sledge Nelson, born January 10, 1872.
II. Hiram Lucius Nelson, born November 12, 1874; married, September 18, 1895, Hattie Hines. Issue: Henry Nelson.
III. Allison Nelson, born June 26, 1876.
IV. Baylis E. Nelson, born March 19, 1878; died November 19, 1898.
V. John Alston Nelson, born March 9, 1881.
VI. Kate Nelson, born January, 1883.
VII. Harvey Nelson, born March, 1888.
VIII. Lovie Nelson, born October 1, 1891.

143. Alston Hunter Greene married, October 17, 1883, Mary Lou Hunnicutt, born May 8, 1860. Issue: Edgar Laurence, Fannie Letitia, and Calvin Clay Greene.

144. William Daniel Greene married, August 30, 1892, Mrs. Edmonia Long Harney, born May 2, 1868. Issue: Evelyn Goodwin and Carl Elkin Greene.

145. Clement Clay Greene married, November 18, 1891, Mae Rhodes, born March 2, 1870; died June 20, 1895.

146. Anna Blanche Greene married, October 17, 1883, Forrest Adair, born March 24, 1864. Reside in Atlanta, Georgia. Issue:

I. Elizabeth Adair, born January 30, 1885.
II. Frank Adair, born July 31, 1886.
III. Forrest Adair, junior, born July 6, 1888.
IV. Robin Adair, born August 14, 1893.

147. Mary Frances Greene married, February 28, 1889, George Townes Rowland, born October 7, 1858. Issue: Hugh (deceased) and Mary Frances Rowland.

---

148. Mary Emma Greene married, October 7, 1873, McKinsie Obediah Thompson, born February 1, 1850. Issue:

      I. ROBERT LYLE THOMPSON, born November 3, 1874; married, June 18, 1893, Eva Eugenia Hilburn. Issue: Lyle A. and Jennie E. Thompson.

     II. ALLISON MCKINSIE THOMPSON, born May 7, 1876.

    III. LEONARD OLIN THOMPSON, born June 12, 1878.

    IV. HELEN LOUISE THOMPSON, born October, 1879.

     V. WILLIAM HUGH THOMPSON, born March 30, 1882; died January 11, 1883.

---

149. Allison Lawson Greene married, April 19, 1882, Susan Caryl Rosenbury. Issue: Charles Allison, Charlotte Louise, Earle Rosenbury, Caryl, and Ward Storrs Greene.

---

150. Horatio W. Bruce, of Louisville, Kentucky, read law with Honorable Leander M. Cox, of Flemingsburg, Kentucky, and was admitted to the bar in 1851; elected Commonwealth's Attorney of the Tenth Judicial District of Kentucky, which office he held until his removal to Louisville in 1858. In 1862 he was elected a Representative from Kentucky in the Confederate Congress,

and served in that body until it was dissolved by the fortunes of war. At the close of the war he returned to Louisville and resumed the practice of law. In 1868 he was elected Circuit Judge of the Ninth Judicial District of Kentucky, and in 1873 became Chancellor of the Louisville Chancery Court by appointment. He was soon afterward elected to that office to fill out an unexpired term, and in 1874 was re-elected for a full term of six years. In 1880 he resigned to accept the attorneyship of the Louisville & Nashville Railroad Company, which position he still holds. He was married in 1856 to Elizabeth Hardin Helm, a daughter of John L. and Lucinda Barbour Helm, of " Helm Place," Hardin County, Kentucky. Issue :

195.   I. HELM BRUCE.
    II. ELIZABETH BARBOUR BRUCE.
    III. MARIA PRESTON POPE BRUCE.
    IV. MARY BRUCE ; married Thomas Floyd Smith.
    V. ALEXANDER BRUCE ; married Sara Moore Van Meter.

---

152. Nancy A. Moran, born October 1, 1813 ; married, May 8, 1831, Nathaniel Purviance Rogers, born September 15, 1807, son of William Rogers and his wife, Ann Cornick, daughter of Richard Cornick and his wife, Olivette Phelps, the daughter of John and Ann Phelps, and the granddaughter of John Phelps (Test. 1772) and

Ann, his wife, of Bedford County, Virginia. The Cornicks were a prominent and influential family of Princess Anne County, Virginia. William Rogers, the father of Nathaniel, was a man of superior attainment and nobility of character, an earnest Christian, and for many years an elder in the Old Cane Ridge Church, Bourbon County, Kentucky, of which his father was a founder, and in which his descendants have been officers for nearly a hundred years. Nancy (Moran) Rogers died December 11, 1846. N. P. Rogers married (2) Mrs. Mary Baylis. No issue. He died February 28, 1863. Issue:

196.   I. CAROLINE A. ROGERS, born July 13, 1833.

197.   II. WILLIAM E. ROGERS, of St. Paul, Minnesota, born August 12, 1835.

       III. JOHN J. ROGERS, born October 16, 1837; died 1897; married (1) Mary E. Bayless, born October 27, 1844; died March 9, 1881. Issue: John J. Rogers; died September 8, 1878. Married (2) Jane Harris. Issue: Martha Hendricks and John J. Rogers.

198.   IV. WARREN THOMAS ROGERS, born December 4, 1839; my friend and comrade.

       V. ALEXANDER N. ROGERS, born April 27, 1843; died young.

       VI. NANCY MARIA ROGERS, born September 6, 1845; died young.

———

153. Rebecca Barber Moran, born August 25, 1815, died February 9, 1893; married, March 11, 1838, Samuel Hedges, of Cane Ridge, Bourbon County, Kentucky, son of Joseph Hedges, the Revolutionary soldier, and

grandson of Charles Hedges, of Frederick County, Maryland, who was the son of Joseph Hedges, the emigrant, who settled in Chester County, Pennsylvania. Samuel Hedges was born June 24, 1792, and died July 3, 1874. Issue :

I. HENRIETTA HEDGES ; married Joseph H. Ewalt December 10, 1863, and had Joseph Hedges Ewalt, born July 15, 1865, and Lily Ewalt, born April 20, 1869, who died in Brooklyn, New York, November 15, 1885.

II. JOSEPH E. HEDGES, born August 12, 1841 ; was Lieutenant in Company C, Ninth Kentucky Cavalry, of the Confederate Army, serving under General Joseph E. Johnston. Married Sallie B. Bedford, and has Bedford Hedges and Mary R. Hedges, who married Junius Clay and has Mary Hedges Clay.

III. LETITIA CLAY HEDGES, a charter member of the "Jemima Johnson" Chapter of the Daughters of the American Revolution.

IV. EDWARD B. HEDGES, born October 6, 1849 ; married Marianne Hildreth, January 13, 1879, and has one daughter, Sallie J. Hedges.

---

154. Elizabeth Jane Moran was born February 24, 1819, and died January 7, 1886. She married, July 12, 1838, Harvey Addison Rogers, born November 7, 1812, and died September 15, 1866. He was a man of fine intellect, cool, ripe judgment, and a generous heart, consequently a man of prominence and influence in the community. To them were born ten children :

I. Edward Benjamin Rogers, born August 8, 1839; died unmarried October 25, 1865.

II. Nathaniel Cobbs Rogers, born April 24, 1841; married Mollie F. Roseberry, born September 25, 1849, daughter of Hiram M. and Caroline (Hildreth) Roseberry, of "Ellerslie," October 1, 1867. She died January, 1897, and left one son:

    I. Roseberry Rogers, born June, 1869; married, May 6, 1890, Ida Barton, and has one son, Barton H. Rogers, born April 2, 1892.

III. Sarah Jane Rogers, born October 1, 1843; married, January 24, 1899 (as his second wife), Thomas M. Parrish, of Midway, Kentucky.

IV. Bettie Gano Rogers, born April 6, 1846; married, May 4, 1870, William H. Prewitt, son of Nelson ———— Prewitt. Issue:

    I. Edward Rogers Prewitt, born April 30, 1871.
    II. Anna Goff Prewitt, born September 18, 1873; married Thomas Kennedy January 30, 1894.
    III. Harvey Moran Prewitt, born January 23, 1875.

V. Nannie R. Rogers, born April 21, 1848; died January 23, 1874; unmarried.

VI. Harvey Allen Rogers, born February 26, 1850; married, January 11, 1876, Nettie Gaitskill, daughter of John and Frances (Branham) Gaitskill. Issue:

    I. John Gaitskill Rogers, born October 19, 1876.
    II. Jane Moran Rogers, born April 20, 1882.
    III. Frank Allen Rogers, born May 10, 1886.

VII. Purviance Rogers, born February 8, 1853; died July 8, 1860.

VIII. Warren Moran Rogers, of "Mt. Auburn," born November 27, 1855; married, January 30, 1894, in New Britain, Connecticut, Frances Fitch, daughter of Frank and ———— Gant Fitch. Issue:

    I. Fielding Gant Rogers, born December 28, 1894.
    II. Harriett Howell Rogers, born December 11, 1897.

IX. Mary Eliza Rogers, born January 27, 1858; married, October 25, 1882, John I. Fisher, son of Ambrose Fisher and his wife, Frances Rogers, daughter of Reverend Samuel and Elizabeth (Irvine) Rogers, and granddaughter of Ezekiel and Rebecca Williamson Rogers, of Charlotte County, Virginia. Reverend Samuel Rogers was a soldier of the War of 1812, and Ezekiel was a soldier of the Revolution, present at the battle of Cowpens, the siege of York, and witnessed the surrender of Cornwallis. Mary Eliza Rogers Fisher died September 26, 1895, leaving three children :

 I. Warren Rogers Fisher, born August 18, 1884.

 II. Elizabeth Prewitt Fisher, born June 22, 1888.

 III. Mary Bennett Fisher, born September 22, 1895.

X. Louis Ray Rogers was born November 5, 1866, and married, April 20, 1894, Iva Dee Allen, daughter of J. G. and Mary (Miller) Allen. They have :

 I. Harvey Allen Rogers, born February 5, 1895.

 II. Julian Grosjean Rogers, born November 11, 1897.

---

155. Henry Clay, born 1819, married Susan Fleece and moved to Hendricks County, Indiana. He has a large and influential family. Issue :

 I. Arabella Clay (Mrs. O. H. Waters).

 II. Mary Catherine Clay (Mrs. Thomas Rose).

 III. Samuel Clinton Clay.

 IV. James Clay.

 V. Sally Clay.

 VI. Crittenden Clay.

 VII. Joseph Clay.

 VIII. Arthur Clay.

156. Olivia Maccoun Clay, daughter of Colonel L. B. and Arabella (Maccoun) Clay, was born January 13, 1823, and married William A. Fleming April 2, 1846. He was born January 13, 1823, and died December 27, 1886. She died February 24, 1888. They lived and died at Pleasant Hill, Missouri. Issue:

> I. AMELIA FLEMING, born March 21, 1847; married, March 16, 1868, Adam C. Travis, a prominent insurance man of St. Louis, who died August 5, 1882. Issue: Olive May Travis (Mrs. S. F. Giles), William Clarke Travis, and Harry J. Travis.
> II. JAMES D. FLEMING was born August 20, 1849; married Eugenia, daughter of Arthur and Melonia (Byng) Nelson and granddaughter of Judge Madison Nelson, of Fredericksburg, Maryland. Issue: Eugenia.

157. Samuel Clay, junior, born April 19, 1825, was for more than half a century one of the most energetic and enterprising business men of Bourbon and Fayette counties, but as the result of an accident has been an invalid for some years past. Though a great sufferer, his patient endurance and fortitude demand the admiration of the household. On the maternal side he is the great-grandson of Reverend David Rice, "the Father of the Presbyterian Church in Kentucky," who was one of the founders of Hampden–Sidney College, Virginia, and of Transylvania (now Kentucky) University. Mr. Rice was a grand, good man, whose life was spent in the cause of

humanity. He married in Pennsylvania Mary, daughter of Reverend Samuel Blair, of Faggs manor, who founded there the Classical and Theological School for the education of the Presbyterian clergy, out of which grew the College of New Jersey, later Princeton University. Samuel Blair (1712–1751) married Frances, daughter of Judge Lawrence Van Hook and his wife, Johanna Smit, daughter of Hendrick Barentse Smit, from Lochen, Holland, a soldier in the West India Company in New Netherlands. Hendrick Barentse Schmidt married Gerritze Willemse, from Niew Kerck (New York), May 11, 1655, and was a magistrate under the Dutch Government for Boshwych, Long Island. (Original copy of will in Book No. 1, Kings County, New York.) Judge Lawrence Van Hook was the son of Arent Isaacszen Van Hook, one of the signers of a petition to Stuyvesant to surrender New Netherlands to the English, on September 5, 1664.

Samuel Clay, junior, married, May 23, 1860, Mary Katharine Rogers, daughter of Captain William S. Rogers and his wife, Henrietta Roseberry, daughter of Hugh Roseberry and his wife, Mary Parker, daughter of Captain Thomas and Mary (Taylor) Parker, of Snow Hill, Maryland. Captain Rogers was born September 30, 1819, and his wife January 26, 1820. They were married May 23, 1839, by Elder John A. Gano. He was the son of William Rogers and his wife, Katherine Skillman, daughter of Christopher and Henrietta (Payne) Skillman, of Loudon County, Virginia, who came to Kentucky about 1804. William Rogers, senior, born in Campbell County, Virginia, July 7, 1784, died February 15, 1862. He was the son of Nathaniel Rogers, born in Charlotte County, Virginia, July 25, 1755, who was a soldier of the Revolution, and moved to Kentucky in 1797 and settled at Caneridge, dying December 22, 1804. Nathaniel Rogers was a member of the Constitutional Convention of Kentucky in 1799. He married Frances, daughter of Colonel Charles and Anne (Walton) Cobbs, August 14, 1783, in Campbell County, Virginia. She died September 20, 1790. Samuel and Mary Rogers Clay have issue :

> I. BELLE CLAY, born March 14, 1861 ; married, November 16, 1881, William Lee Lyons, born June 3, 1857, son of Henry J. Lyons and his wife, Laura Simmons, daughter of Matilda Ann Lee and William Simmons, and granddaughter of Wilford Lee and Rebecca Hill, who were married August 2, 1796, by Reverend John Carman. Rebecca Hill was the daughter of Judge Atkinson Hill, of Bardstown, Kentucky. Mr. Lyons is an active business man, and was for many years a member of the City Council, serving as its President, and again as Chairman of the Committee on Finance. During a six months' absence of Mayor Charles D. Jacob he acted as Mayor pro tem., being elected to that position by the Council under circumstances which made

the compliment a very flattering one. He is President of the Board of Public Safety under the present administration. W. L. and Belle Clay Lyons have issue:

    I. SAMUEL CLAY LYONS.

    II. LAURA SIMMONS LYONS.

    III. MARY ROGERS LYONS.

    IV. WILLIAM LEE LYONS, JUNIOR.

II. WILLIAM ROGERS CLAY, born November 9, 1864, was graduated from Kentucky University in 1885; from Georgetown University, D. C., with degree of Bachelor of Law in 1888 and Master of Law in 1889; Private Secretary to Senator James B. Beck from 1887-90; in 1891 was elected Superintendent of the Public Schools of Lexington, Kentucky, which office he still holds, while continuing the practice of law.

III. BISHOP CLAY, born October 18, 1866; married Lucy Chenault, daughter of Anderson and Margaret Oldham Chenault, of Montgomery County, Kentucky, a descendant of William Chenault and Matthew Mullins, of Revolutionary fame.

IV. SAMUEL BLAIR CLAY, born December 4, 1873; married, November 7, 1893, Helen Madge, only daughter of Professor Albert and Catherine (Howe) Coburn, of Glasgow, Scotland.

---

158. Elizabeth Rice Clay (third child of Colonel L. B. and Arabella (Maccoun) Clay) was born in 1826 and married (first) her own cousin, William Clay, son of George and America (Bainbridge) Clay, of St. Louis. She married (second) George D. Doughty, son of George Daniel and —— (Hamm) Doughty, of Rochester, New York. George D. Doughty, senior, was a soldier of the War of 1812, and present at the storming of Quebec. Issue:

I. ANNIE DOUGHTY; married Thomas Benton Allen in December, 1870, and has issue: Hugh C. Allen, Robert G. Allen, George B. Allen, Katie M. Allen, and James Allen.

II. KATE DOUGHTY; married Robert Maccoun, son of Ward Maccoun, of Hendricks County, Indiana, and has two children, Annie and Jack. Annie Maccoun married William Neville, and has two children: Adie Neville and Glen Neville.

III. PHILIP G. DOUGHTY; died unmarried.

IV. GEORGE DOUGHTY.

---

159. John Ward Clay, born February 20, 1823; died November 7, 1879. Married (first) June 16, 1846, Mary Anderson, born April 3, 1830; died September 16, 1855. Married (second) September 7, 1858, Nannie C. Owings, who died May 26, 1871. Issue:

I. ALBERT ANDERSON CLAY, born June 17, 1847; married (1) November, 1871, Nettie Owings. Issue: Mary A. Clay. Married (2) Emma Wilkerson. Issue.

II. MARY B. (Dead.)

III. JULIAN WARD CLAY, born 1852.

IV. JOSIAH CLAY. (Dead.)

V. LUCY O. CLAY, born June 8, 1859.

VI. JOHN W. CLAY, born September 21, 1860; married, April, 1888, Lizzie Bridges. Issue: William Caldwell Clay.

VII. M. C. CLAY, born 1863; married, December 14, 1886, Lula Fesler. Issue: Elizabeth Clay.

VIII. GREEN CLAY, born September 29, 1866.

---

160. Samuel Edward Clay, born July 10, 1825, died September 11, 1892, at the Eastern Lunatic Asylum, at Lexington, Kentucky. Married Amanda F. Phelps, born January 22, 1842. Issue:

26

I. MARY ELIZA CLAY; married September 6, 1893, James T. Highland.
II. SALLIE CLAY.
III. MARGARET B. CLAY.
IV. ANN CLAY.
V. S. E. CLAY.
VI. W. P. CLAY.

161. Captain Harry P. Bedford, born April 10, 1826; enlisted and served throughout the Mexican War; was Captain of Company C, Fifth Cavalry, Confederate States Army, for three years during the Civil War; married, March, 1853, Mary, daughter of Samuel Ewalt, of Bourbon County. Issue:

I. ELIZABETH W. BEDFORD; married Daniel Shawhan. Issue.
II. THOMAS BEDFORD.
III. EWALT BEDFORD.
IV. ANNIE PUGH BEDFORD; married John Lovely. Issue.
V. HARRY BEDFORD.
VI. WILLIAM B. BEDFORD.
VII. BENJAMIN BEDFORD.
VIII. MARY H. BEDFORD.
IX. ELEANOR B. BEDFORD.

162. Anna Gist married David Howell, born 1798; died 1874, the eighth David Howell in direct succession from Welsh parentage. He was the son of David (and —— Hukill) Howell, who was a soldier in the War of 1812, enlisting at sixteen years of age. Their children were:

I. Elizabeth Howell, born 1835; married Robert Prewitt, son of William C. Prewitt, and grandson of Robert Prewitt, who came from Virginia to Fayette County, Kentucky, about 1794, in which year General Anthony Wayne's decisive victory over the Indians at the Miami Rapids put a complete stop to the savage forays by which the Kentucky settler had up to this time been harassed. That bold expedition, with the bold action which was its result, was shared in by many a gallant soldier from Fayette County. William C. Prewitt died in 1854. His wife was Margaret Edmonson, daughter of Captain John Edmonson, one of the many brave Kentuckians killed on the 22d of January, 1813. Issue:

  I. Howell Prewitt; married Lily Chenault. Issue.

  II. Robert Prewitt.

  III. William Prewitt.

  IV. Margaret Prewitt; married W. G. Thornbury.

  V. Anna Prewitt.

  VI. Elizabeth Prewitt.

  VII. Alma Prewitt; married Doctor Blanding.

II. Susan Howell, born 1838; married William A. Hood. Issue:

  I. Anna Hood; married W. A. DeHaven.

  II. Theodocia Hood; married Doctor George Warner.

  III. Florence Hood; married —— Donelson, of Tennessee.

  IV. Leah Hood; married —— Reese.

  V. Kate Hood.

  VI. John Hood.

  VII. William Hood.

  VIII. Richard Hood.

III. David Howell, born 1840; married Katherine Gay. Issue:

  I. David Howell; married Miss Berkely.

  II. Robert Howell.

  III. Oliver Howell.

  IV. William Howell.

IV. Rezin Gist Howell, born 1842; married Emily Ayres. Issue: Anna Howell and Mary Howell.

V. Howard Cecil Howell, born 1846; married Lily Ashbrook. Issue: Cecil, Grace, and Clifford Howell.

VI. Clayton Howell, born 1848; married Harriet Fitch. Issue: Rezin, Clayton, Harry, and Frances Howell.

VII. FLORENCE HOWELL, born 1851; married Reverend D. J. Ditzler. Issue : Mary Ditzler, married Andrew Cropper ; Annette and Florence Ditzler.

VIII. HENRIETTA HOWELL, born 1860 ; married Jere E. Rogers. Issue : Anna Gist, Fanny, Florence, and Clark Rogers.

---

163. Rachel E. Gist, born 1826, married James Turner. Issue :

1. DAWSON TURNER ; married F. R. Matthews. Issue :

    I. ELIZABETH MATTHEWS ; married Clarence Whistler.

    II. ELEANOR MATTHEWS ; married Edward Bedford, junior. (See 82.)

---

165. Patsy Chandler Prewitt married John H. Goff, of Indian Fields, Clark County, Kentucky. Issue :

I. THOMAS GOFF ; married Mary Suddeth, and has Anna, Carrie, and Suddeth Goff.

II. HENRIETTA C. GOFF ; married Archie Bedford, of Bourbon County, and has John, Caswell, and Mattie Bedford.

III. LEVI GOFF ; married Julia Bedford, and has six children.

IV. WILLIAM GOFF ; died unmarried.

V. EMMA GOFF ; married Woodson Browning, and has four children.

VI. ELISHA GOFF ; married (1) Ada Bruton, (2) —— Mitchell.

VII. JOHN GOFF ; married Betty Gardner, of Mississippi, and has two children.

VIII. CASWELL PREWITT GOFF ; married (1) Agnes Chenault, of Richmond, (2) Mary Evans, of Clark County, and has one child.

IX. JAMES PREWITT GOFF ; married Mina Hon, and has one child.

X. PATTY GOFF ; married John R. Downing, of Mason County, and has one son.

XI. MARGARET GOFF.

XII. STROTHER GOFF ; died young.

XIII. ELIZABETH B. GOFF ; married Archie Bedford, of Missouri, and has three children.

166. Caswell Prewitt, born September 13, 1842; married, January 19, 1869, Annie Kenney, born December 27, 1847, of Bourbon, a descendant of Captain Thomas Skillman, an early settler of Long Island.   Issue:

    I. SMITH KENNEY PREWITT; died in infancy.
    II. CLIFTON R. PREWITT, born April 20, 1872.
    III. MARY DAWSON PREWITT, born December 13, 1873; married Dawson W. Thurston, January 2, 1894, and resides in Minneapolis, Minnesota, and has Stella, Anna Louise, and D. W. Thurston, junior.
    IV. JOSIAH PREWITT; died in infancy.
    V. PATTY C. PREWITT, born August 11, 1877.
    VI. EUGENE CHARLES PREWITT, born November 19, 1881.
    VII. WILMOTT KENNEY PREWITT, born June 24, 1884.
    VIII. HENRY CLAY PREWITT, born May 25, 1887.
    IX. ANNIE CASWELL PREWITT, born May 1, 1890.

167. Allen Prewitt married Mary Vance Ried.   Issue:

    I. HENRY R. PREWITT; married (1) Keturah Green; (2) Ann Atkinson, of Hill City, Kansas, who left one child; (3) Katie Grubbs, of Mt. Sterling.
    II. FLORENCE PREWITT; married Frank Jackson, of Winchester, Kentucky, December, 1889, and has Allen Prewitt and Josiah Jackson.
    III. HENRIETTA PREWITT; married Charleton Evans, and has Florence Ray, Thomas J., and Allen Prewitt Evans.
    IV. MARCUS A. PREWITT; married Jennie Evans in 1896.
    V. ELLA R. PREWITT.
    VI. RICHARD RIED PREWITT.
    VII. JULIA PREWITT.

168. Clifton Prewitt married, in 1870, Nannie Wilson, and has:

    I. JAMES WILSON PREWITT, born September, 1871.
    II. WILLIAM CASWELL PREWITT, born March, 1873.
    III. LIZZIE H. PREWITT ; died in 1890, aged sixteen years.
    IV. DANIEL JONES PREWITT, born February, 1876 ; married, September, 1896, Alys Burton, of Mt. Sterling, Kentucky.
    V. ALLEN GANO PREWITT, born December, 1880.
    VI. JOHN McGARVEY PREWITT.
    VII. LEILA H. PREWITT.
    VIII. WENONA PREWITT ; died in infancy.

169. Mattie B. Kennedy, born September 14, 1817 ; married October 29, 1835, Charles Todd Garrard, born June 13, 1812; died February 23, 1873, son of General James and Nancy (Lewis) Garrard and grandson of Governor James Garrard, of Kentucky. Mattie B. Kennedy died January 28, 1876. Issue:

    I. EDWARD D. GARRARD ; married Fannie Field, of Missouri, and left one son, French Field Garrard, who married, October, 1898, Kate Oliver, of Dallas, Texas. Edward died in Texas in 1876.
    II. JULIA CLAY GARRARD ; married John W. Sparks, of Harrison County, Kentucky, and has seven children : Charles, Mattie, Lillie, James, Bettie, Jessie, and William.
    III. SARAH RUSSELL GARRARD ; married Thomas A. Nichols, of Harrison County, and died August, 1894, at Kansas City, Missouri, leaving four children : Charles, Belle, Annie, and Brown Nichols.
    IV. MARY GARRARD ; married Doctor James C. Bierbower, of Maysville, Kentucky, and has three sons : Charles Garrard, James, and Richard Bierbower.
    V. JAMES GARRARD.
    VI. BRUTUS CLAY GARRARD ; married Marian Walker, and has : Walker, Terry, Russell, Jessie, and Edna.

VII. Annie M. Garrard; married C. A. Daugherty September
    1, 1870, and has Charles Garrard, James, Edward,
    Frank, Garrard, Helen, and Annie.
VIII. Charles T. Garrard, junior.
IX. John Garrard.

---

170. Patsy Kennedy, born 1830; married, in 1849,
Ossian Edwards, born in 1827, died in 1869, son of
Major John Edwards and his second wife, Elizabeth,
daughter of Captain John Kellar. Major Edwards died
in 1853, aged ninety-two. His wife lived to be seventy-
eight. Patsy and Ossian Edwards had issue:

I. Bettie Edwards; married Walter S. Blaisdell; (2) John
    W. McIlvain. No issue.
II. Julia Edwards.
III. Alice Edwards; married Thompson Ware, and has James,
    Edward, and Pattie Ware.
IV. Ossian Edwards; married Alice Patton.
V. John Edwards; died at the age of thirty-three.
VI. Mattie Edwards; married Walter Clark.

---

171. James Garrard Bedford, of Monroe County,
Missouri, died August 15, 1886; married May 29, 1860,
Nannie B. Holliday. Issue:

I. Edwin V. Bedford.
II. Thomas H. Bedford; married Anna Washburne. Issue:
    Lola, James E., and Orville Bedford.
III. Mary O. Bedford; married W. P. Jones. Issue: Morris
    B. Jones.
IV. James G. Bedford, junior; married Lina Bowles. Issue:
    George Nichols and Mary Grace Bedford.
V. Nellie Bedford.
VI. Addie H. Bedford.
VII. Edwin Bedford; died young.

172. Jeptha D. Bedford, born December 12, 1837; married (first), September 11, 1860, Annie E. Hall, born April 18, 1842; married (second), November 11, 1875, Armadilla Toland, of Illinois. Issue:

  I. ANN DUDLEY BEDFORD, born December 12, 1861; married, February 25, 1885, Joseph E. Bird, of Billings, Missouri. Issue: Elmer and Laurie Bird.
  II. JAMES F. BEDFORD, of Afton, Indian Territory, born March 12, 1866.
  III. FRANCES E. BEDFORD, born July 13, 1877.

173. Sallie Maria Bedford married R. M. Martin, of Winchester, Kentucky, later of Paris, Missouri. Issue:

  I. JOHN MARTIN, of Kansas City; married Lou V. Eib. Issue: John N. and Runcie Martin.
  II. JAMES B. MARTIN, of Louisville; married Kate Haggard, of Clark County, Kentucky.
  III. CARTER N. MARTIN, of Winchester; married Nannie Owen. Issue: Charles C., Allie B., Lillie N., and Mary B. Martin.
  IV. ELIZABETH B. MARTIN; married (1) G. W. Glenn, of Missouri; (2) C. B. Todd, of Winchester, Kentucky. Issue: George N. and Etta F. Glenn.

174. Benjamin F. Bedford, of Bourbon County, married Elizabeth, daughter of Silas and Parmelia Quisenberry Evans, of Fayette County. Issue:

  I. CARRIE MORAN BEDFORD; married Nathan Bayles, junior, son of Nathan and Rebecca (Roseberry) Bayles. Issue: Elizabeth Bayles.
  II. SILAS E. BEDFORD; married Margaret E. Gaitskill. (See 84.)
  III. RICHARD E. BEDFORD.
  IV. BENJAMIN BEDFORD.

175. Nancy Lewis Bedford married, September 3, 1872, Doctor J. L. Connelly, of Harristown, Illinois. Issue: Maggie P. (died young), Sue H., George, John L., Alice B., and Laura W. Connelly.

---

176. Margaret T. Bedford, born March 4, 1840; married, September 20, 1860, James H. Pickrell, of Springfield, Illinois. Issue:

I. NANNIE PICKRELL; died in infancy.
II. AMANDA W. PICKRELL, born December 28, 1862; married, October, 1889, D. Howard Crutcher, of Chicago. Issue: Helen, Ruth, and Marshall Crutcher.
III. ANNIE LAURA PICKRELL; married, December 30, 1890, Reverend Charles Medbury. Issue: Margaret and Sheldon P. Medbury.
IV. HELEN PICKRELL; died young.
V. HARVEY PICKRELL; married, June 15, 1897, Edith Styles Munger.
VI. WILLIAM BENJAMIN PICKRELL, of Chicago.
VII. JESSE G. PICKRELL; died young.
VIII. MAGGIE RUSSELL PICKRELL; married, December 22, 1896, Charles H. Jones.
IX. HENRY A. PICKRELL.
X. SCOTT W. PICKRELL.
XI. HATHAWAY PICKRELL, died young.

---

177. Elizabeth Buckner married, February, 1840, John T. Woodford, born August 26, 1812, a lineal descendant of Major William Woodford, the immigrant, who married as his third wife Ann Cocke (September 3, 1732), daugh-

27

ter of Doctor William and Elizabeth Catesby Cocke.
Doctor William Cocke was Secretary of State in 1712–14;
a member of the Council, 1715; and Commander-in-
chief of Warwick and James City counties. John T.
Woodford was a successful farmer of Bourbon County,
and died but a few years since. Mrs. Woodford is still
living, a blessing in the homes of her children. With her
generation passes a beautiful type of Kentucky womanhood. Issue :

> I. SALLIE WOODFORD ; married Captain E. F. Spears, a gal-
> lant soldier of the " Lost Cause," a son of Abram and
> Rebecca (Ford) Spears, of Paris, Kentucky. Issue :
>> I. MARY SPEARS.
>> II. JOHN W. SPEARS ; married Elizabeth Stephens.
>> Issue : Edward and Charles Spears.
>> III. ELIZABETH SPEARS.
>> IV. CATESBY SPEARS.
>> V. KEITH YOUNG SPEARS.
>
> II. MARY LETITIA WOODFORD ; married Colonel E. F. Clay, of
> Runnymede, Bourbon County. (See 129.)
>
> III. BUCKNER WOODFORD, Paris, Kentucky; married Nannie
> Brooks. Issue : John, Elizabeth, Samuel, and Buckner
> Woodford.
>
> IV. JOHN T. WOODFORD, of Mt. Sterling, Kentucky, born August,
> 1847 ; married, February 13, 1872, Nannie, daughter of
> Anderson and Margaret (Oldham) Chenault, of Mont-
> gomery. Issue : Margaret, Thornton, Catesby, Chenault,
> William, and Lucy Clay Woodford.
>
> V. BETTIE WOODFORD ; married Henry, son of Jacob and Eliz-
> abeth (Cook) Spears. Issue : Jacob, Elizabeth, John,
> and Lee Spears.
>
> VI. CATESBY WOODFORD, of Bourbon County ; married Amelia,
> daughter of Henry and Martha (Clay) Davenport, of
> Virginia.

VII. HENRY WOODFORD, of Mt. Sterling, Kentucky; married
Lelia Bush. Issue: Mary Grant, Buckner, Elizabeth,
Margaret, and Kelly Woodford.

VIII. BENJAMIN WOODFORD, of Bourbon County, born October 24,
1856; married, October 29, 1879, Alice, daughter of
Samuel and Elvira (Scott) Brooks. Issue: Benjamin,
James, Mary, William, Scott, Brooks, and John T.
Woodford.

IX. MARIA WOODFORD; married Professor William Yerkes, of
Paris, Kentucky, an educator of note. Issue: John,
Amanda, and Elizabeth McKnight Yerkes.

---

178. Elizabeth Payne Lewis married, February 11,
1851, Colonel Henry C. Howard. Issue:

I. MARY BULLOCK HOWARD; married Reverend Dudley Powers,
of the Protestant Episcopal Church.
II. ANNE M. HOWARD; married J. O. Embry.
III. DOCTOR DOUGLAS LEWIS HOWARD; died April 30, 1889.
IV. HENRY CLAY HOWARD, Judge of the Bourbon County Court;
married Margaret Helm Clay. (See 83.)

---

179. Margaret Helm Lewis married Moses C. Chapline, of a prominent colonial family of Virginia. Issue:
Lewis Loring, Elizabeth Lewis, and Mary Loring Chapline.

---

180. Mary Letitia Lewis married Frank R. Armstrong. Issue:

I. JOSEPH ARMSTRONG; married Lillian Metcalf. Issue.
II. DOUGLAS ARMSTRONG.
III. FRANK ARMSTRONG.
IV. BESSIE ARMSTRONG.
V. CASSIUS ARMSTRONG.
VI. ISABEL ARMSTRONG.

181. Margaret Thomas married Doctor Isaac McCloskey. Issue :

> I. KATE McCLOSKEY; married (1) William Mitchell; (2) Judge
> A. P. Harcourt. Issue :
>> I. STELLA MITCHELL; married Robert Van Dyke.
>> Issue : William Mitchell Van Dyke.
>> II. MARGARET MITCHELL; married John Throckmorton
>> Bate, son of Clarence Smalley and Octavia
>> (Zantzinger) Bate, a lineal descendant of
>> Governor Spotswood, and of the prominent
>> Moore, Robinson, and Throckmorton families
>> of Virginia. Issue : Margaret Mitchell and
>> John T. Bate.
>> III. ASHTON P. HARCOURT.
>> IV. ISAAC M. HARCOURT.
>> V. SUSAN HARCOURT; married Robert Lee Thomas,
>> son of State Senator Captain James M. Thomas,
>> of Bourbon County, and his wife, Annie E.
>> Rogers, a lineal descendant of Thomas Dud-
>> ley, Governor of Massachusetts, 1634–50.
>> VI. RITA HARCOURT.

---

182. Henry Clay Thomas, born August 15, 1833 ;
married, May 15, 1866, Marietta Coke, of Bardstown,
Kentucky. Issue :

> I. ARCHIE THOMAS.
> II. W. G. THOMAS; married, July 4, 1894, Jessie Jenkins.

---

183. Stephen Osborne Southall, B. L., LL. D., born
in Jamestown, Virginia, December 16, 1816 ; was graduated in 1841 from the Law School of the University of

Virginia ; in 1852–3 represented Prince Edward County in the House of Delegates ; was elected July, 1864, Commonwealth's Attorney, but having little taste for political life, resigned in 1866 to accept a call to fill the Chair of Law in the University of Virginia, where he died November 28, 1884.

---

184. Philip Francis Southall, M. D., born April 6, 1822, died October 6, 1898 ; was the leading physician of Amelia County, Virginia, for many years. As a Magistrate and as a chairman of his political party he rendered important service. It is said of him, "as a companion, a guest, a host, a charming anecdotist and conversationalist, he was one of the most accomplished men of southside Virginia." In 1845 he married Eliza J. Goode, daughter of Colonel Robert and Mary Hatfield (Loper or Lepere) Goode. Issue :

199.   I. Philip Turner Southall, M. D.
200.   II. Robert Goode Southall.
201.   III. Stephen Osborne Southall.
        IV. Mary E. Southall.

---

185. Speed Smith Goodloe died May 14, 1877 ; was for many years Judge of the Lexington City Court, and was a man whose genial manners and kind disposition

drew around him a host of devoted friends. He married Mary E., daughter of T. T. and Eliza A. Rogers Shreve, of Louisville. Issue :

     I. LILA GOODLOE ; married Thomas, son of William G. and Sarah (McConnell) Moore, and grandson of Captain John Moore, an early pioneer of Fayette County, Kentucky. Issue : Marie Moore.

     II. SALLIE GOODLOE ; died young.

     III. SPEED GOODLOE ; married Rose Cebro, of Parkersburg, West Virginia.

     IV. SHREVE GOODLOE.

     V. MAMIE GOODLOE.

     VI. MADELLE GOODLOE ; married Harry J., son of Henry J. and Laura Simmons Lyons. (See 157.) Issue : Mary Shreve and Madelle Goodloe Lyons.

---

186. Colonel William Cassius Goodloe was born June 27, 1841 ; in 1860 was private secretary to his great-uncle, General Cassius M. Clay, United States Minister to Russia, and for much of the time acted as Secretary of Legation ; in 1862 was commissioned by President Lincoln Captain and Assistant Adjutant General of Volunteers, United States Army, and was brevetted for gallant service on the battlefield.

He married, June 8, 1865, Mary E., daughter of Samuel Man, of Manville, Rhode Island, a grandniece of Bishop Brownell, and granddaughter of Jonathan Brownell, of Rhode Island. In 1871 Colonel Goodloe was elected to

the Legislature by the Republicans of Fayette County;
March 4, 1878, was appointed Resident at the Court of
Belgium, where with his family he remained about two
and a half years, the recipient of many personal courtesies
from the King and Queen; in 1880 he resigned and
returned to Kentucky. As an editor and public speaker
Colonel Goodloe used his powers most effectively in
advocating those measures so unpopular at that time in
Kentucky, namely, the admission of negro testimony and
the adoption of the Thirteenth, Fourteenth, and Fifteenth
Amendments to the Federal Constitution. Though an
enthusiastic advocate of his own convictions, Colonel
Goodloe was a generous opponent, having numerous
friends who lamented his untimely death. Mrs. Goodloe
lives quietly at her beautiful home, "Loudoun," near
Lexington, Kentucky. Issue:

    I. MARY MAN GOODLOE; married, November 15, 1888, Thomas
        Clay McDowell. (See 189.)
    II. ANNIE GOODLOE; married, June 30, 1891, Andrew Leonard,
        of Chicago. Issue: Mary Goodloe and Frederick
        Washburne Leonard.
    III. WILHELMINA GOODLOE.
    IV. LOUISE BROWNELL GOODLOE; married, June, 1896, D. Gray
        Falconer.
    V. ELIZABETH LESLIE GOODLOE.
    VI. GRACE GOODLOE.
    VII. WILLIAM CASSIUS GOODLOE.
    VIII. GREEN CLAY GOODLOE.

187. Harry Boyle Clay, a brave and gallant Captain in the Confederate service, married Nannie Bradley Bynum, daughter of Joshua and Louisa (Bradley) Phipps. Issue:

I. HARRY B. CLAY, JUNIOR; married Fanny Russell Neill. Issue: Mary and an infant.
II. ELSIE CLAY; married Henry Clay McDowell, junior.
III. MARY L. CLAY; married William D. Kenner. Issue: Harry Clay, Lanier Neill, Nannie Bradley (deceased), Kenneth, and Elsie Clay Kenner.
IV. IDA H. CLAY.

188. Thomas Hart Clay married Annie Gratz, daughter of Benjamin and Anna Maria Boswell Gratz, granddaughter of Joseph and Judith Gist Boswell, and great-granddaughter of Colonel Nathaniel and Judith Carey Bell Gist.

Mr. Clay was for eleven years one of the associate editors of the Youth's Companion, in Boston, Massachusetts, and is now engaged in the real estate business at Lexington, Kentucky. Issue: Miriam, Anna, and Henrietta Clay.

189. Anne Clay, only surviving child of Colonel Henry Clay, married, May 21, 1857, Henry Clay McDowell, son of William Adair McDowell and his wife, Maria Hawkins Harvey. He was born in Fincastle County, Virginia, in 1832; was graduated at the Louisville Law

School, and won his way to a successful practice in the profession, and was for some years the partner of his brother - in - law, Judge Bland Ballard, of Louisville. He was among the earliest in Kentucky to take up arms for the Union on the breaking out of the Civil War, and was commissioned by President Lincoln as Assistant Adjutant General and served on the staff of General Rosecrans and General Boyle. He was United States Marshal, during Mr. Lincoln's administration, for Kentucky. Some years ago Colonel McDowell purchased "Ashland," the home of Henry Clay, from Kentucky University, and there resides, devoting himself to the care of this beautiful estate and the business of the Lexington & Eastern Railway Company, of which he is President. Issue:

I. NANNETTE McDOWELL; married, April 19, 1892, Doctor Thomas Stapleton Bullock, a successful physician of Louisville. Issue: Henry McDowell Bullock.

II. HENRY CLAY McDOWELL; married, July 5, 1893, Elsie Clay, daughter of Captain Harry Boyle Clay, of Tennessee, son of Thomas Hart Clay, senior.

III. WILLIAM ADAIR McDOWELL; married, October 26, 1887, Alice Dudley, daughter of Right Reverend T. U. Dudley. Issue: William Cochran McDowell.

IV. THOMAS CLAY McDOWELL; married, November 15, 1888, Mary Man Goodloe, daughter of Colonel William Cassius and Mary (Man) Goodloe, of Lexington. Issue: Annie Clay and William Cassius Goodloe McDowell.

V. JULIA PRATHER McDOWELL.

VI. MADELINE McDOWELL; married, November 17, 1898, Lieutenant Desha Breckinridge.

VII. BALLARD McDOWELL, born March 14, 1877; died November 3, 1881.

190. James Brown Clay, junior, enlisted in the Confederate Army in 1862, and served on the staff of General John C. Breckinridge during the greater part of the war. Soon after the battle of Chickamauga he ran the blockade from Wilmington, North Carolina, via Bermuda and Halifax, to Montreal, Canada, reaching there in time to see his father before his death. In the following spring he returned to the Confederacy and rejoined General Breckinridge. When the latter became Secretary of War, Lieutenant Clay joined the staff of General Echols, serving until the close of the war. He married, January 20, 1880, Eliza, daughter of Boone Ingles, of Lexington.

---

191. Henry Clay, born in Lisbon, Portugal, November 19, 1849, was christened on board the United States frigate Independence, flagship of the Mediterranean squadron. He was a member of the Louisville bar, and gave promise of a brilliant career. In 1880 he joined the Howgate Arctic Expedition, which failed, owing to the unseaworthiness of the ship Guluare. He remained in Greenland during the winter of 1880-1, and in the following spring joined the "United States Expedition to Lady Franklin Bay and Grinnell Land" under command of Lieutenant Greely. General Basil W. Duke, in

a tribute to him, says: " His intellectual endowments were
of the highest order. He was one of the bravest men I
ever knew. He was absolutely truthful, entirely sincere,
and perfectly independent in thought and deed. He was
the very incarnation of stainless integrity and romantic
honor. Not for all the 'wealth of Ormus and of Ind'
would he have abandoned a cause or betrayed a conviction."

192. Lieutenant Thomas J. Clay graduated in medicine
in 1873. In 1877 was appointed by President Hayes
Second Lieutenant, United States Army, and in 1883 was
graduated from the Infantry and Cavalry School at
Fort Leavenworth, Kansas. Served in the Geronimo
campaign, and was retired, as First Lieutenant, in 1894,
on account of heart trouble.

193. Captain Charles D. Clay received his appointment
as Second Lieutenant in the Army from President Arthur
in 1883. In 1887 he was graduated from the Infantry
and Cavalry School at Fort Leavenworth, Kansas. He
was promoted to First Lieutenant in 1891. He was the
Regimental Adjutant of the Seventeenth Infantry during
the Santiago campaign, and was in the battle of El Caney,
on July 1st, and in the trenches before Santiago from July
2d to July 17th. He was recommended by his Regimental

and Brigade Commanders for a brevet for "conspicuous courage and coolness and efficiency in transmitting orders under the fire of the enemy." He was promoted Captain, August 15, 1898. ————————

194. Lucretia Hart Clay is a much - interested member of the Daughters of the American Revolution, and was Regent of the Lexington Chapter when it erected and dedicated that beautiful monument to those brave women who so materially aided in the defense of Bryan's Station. This is said to be the first monument erected by women to women. Miss Clay is a fine historian and a ready writer, and was recently elected State Regent of the Daughters of the American Revolution for Kentucky.

————————

195. Helm Bruce, born November 16, 1860, a prominent member of the Louisville bar, was graduated from the Male High School in 1878; from Washington and Lee University in 1880, and from the Louisville Law School in 1882, winning honors in each institution. He married, December 17, 1884, Sallie Hare, daughter of Professor James White, of Washington and Lee University. Issue:

  I. James White Bruce.
  II. Louise Reed Bruce.
  III. Elizabeth Barbour Bruce.
  IV. Helm Bruce, Junior.

196. Caroline A. Rogers, born July, 1833, was a woman of wonderful gentleness and dignity of character. She married, April, 1860, John T. Croxton (son of Henry and Ann (Redman) Croxton), who was graduated with honor from Yale College in 1857; studied law under Governor James Robinson, and began the practice of his profession in Paris, Kentucky, in 1859; was commissioned by President Lincoln Lieutenant Colonel of the Fourth Kentucky, United States Army; served with distinction throughout the Civil War, and rose from one rank to another until he was brevetted Major General; was appointed by President Grant, in 1872, Minister to Bolivia, dying there in 1873. Issue:

    I. HARRY ROGERS CROXTON.
    II. ANNIE DEGUERRA B. CROXTON; married Lucien Logan, of
        Danville, Ky. Issue: Caroline Croxton Logan.

---

197. William Edward Rogers was born August 12, 1835, at Cane Ridge, Bourbon County, Kentucky, and was educated at Bethany College, Virginia; married, June 10, 1857, Margaret Vernon, born June 10, 1840, daughter of Hubbard and Elizabeth (Spears) Vernon, a descendant of Jacob Spears, a Revolutionary soldier. Hubbard Vernon was a grandson of Hubbard Williams, who fought at Stoney Point, Monmouth, and Germantown. William E. and Margaret K. Rogers had issue:

 I. Hubbard Vernon Rogers, born May 16, 1858.

 II. Benjamin F. Rogers, born March 12, 1860; died November 2, 1890; married, November 8, 1881, Kate Newton, daughter of John B. and Lucy (Simms) Wallace. Issue: Wallace F. Rogers (dead), William E. Rogers, and Benjamin F. Rogers.

 III. Elizabeth Moran Rogers, born August 27, 1862; married, September 23, 1884, Samuel, son of Governor Beriah and Ann (Shelby) Magoffin, a descendant of Governor Isaac Shelby. Issue: Vernon Marguerite, Samuel St. Paul, and Elizabeth Rogers Magoffin.

 IV. Nathaniel P. Rogers, born December 17, 1864.

 V. John T. Rogers, born July 18, 1867; was educated at Kentucky University; was graduated with honor from the Medical Department of the University of Minnesota in 1890; spent some time abroad taking special courses in surgery at Edinburgh and Vienna. Is a prominent young surgeon of St. Paul.

 VI. William E. Rogers, Junior, born July 31, 1869; died in North Dakota, August 14, 1892.

 VII. Maggie Kate Rogers, born November 30, 1872; died July 8, 1873.

 VIII. Francis Holton Rogers, born February 3, 1874; died April 18, 1877.

---

198. Warren Thomas Rogers (fourth child of N. P. Rogers) was born December 4, 1839, and died July 17, 1887. He married, March 13, 1868, Louise Evans, daughter of Silas and Parmelia (Quisenberry) Evans, of Fayette County. Issue:

 I. Warren T. Rogers, born April 3, 1869.

 II. Silas Evans Rogers, born May 19, 1871.

 III. Elizabeth Bedford Rogers, born March 30, 1874.

 IV. John Sutton Rogers, born February 7, 1877.

 V. Maggie Vernon Rogers, born March 11, 1879.

VI. CARRIE HANSON ROGERS, born June 15, 1881.
VII. MARY JOHNSON ROGERS, born September 15, 1884.
VIII. JOSEPH BROOKS ROGERS, born October 15, 1887; died
October 26, 1890.

---

199. Philip Turner Southall, M. D., born May 18, 1851.
Entered the Medical School of the University in 1872–3,
and the following year graduated from the Richmond
Medical College. He settled in Amelia, and has an
extensive practice; is a member of the Board of Man-
agers of the Eastern Lunatic Asylum of Virginia.

---

200. Robert Goode Southall, born December 26, 1852;
was graduated in law from the University of Virginia in
1876, and the same year opened his office in Amelia. He
was a delegate to the National Democratic Convention
which met in Chicago in 1884, and also to the Convention held in St. Louis in 1888; has been County Chairman of the Democratic party since 1876; a member of
the Democratic Central Committee since 1883, and Commonwealth's Attorney since 1884.

---

201. Reverend Stephen Osborne Southall, born May
15, 1858; educated at Kenmore High School and the
University of Virginia; was graduated from the Virginia

Theological Seminary in 1889 ; in that year was ordained to the Deaconate by Right Reverend F. M. Whittle, and placed in charge of the churches in Tazewell County ; was ordained Priest in 1890 by Right Reverend A. M. Randolph, and accepted a call to Lunenburg Parish, Richmond County, February 12, 1891. At this time he married Nellie A. Southall, daughter of Captain Frank W. and Ellen (O'Sullivan) Southall. In 1866 he accepted a call to Rocky Mount, Virginia, where he is now living. He is an intelligent genealogist, and has most generously contributed much valuable data to this work, for which he has the sincere thanks of the compiler.

THE CLAY ARMS AND CREST.

SOME ENGLISH DATA OF THE CLAY FAMILY.

The following extract is from the parochial register of Chesterfield, Derbyshire : "January 1687 Robertus Clay et Hannah Slater Nupt. December 1688. Robertus filius Roberte et Hannah uxoris bapt."

In the Parish Church of Crich are some monuments of the family of Clay with quaint epitaphs, in which is a continual play upon the name. The following is from the monument of John Clay, Esquire, who died May, 1632, and Mary, his first wife, daughter of William Calton, Esquire, Chief Cock-matcher and servant to King Henry VIII, who died August 31, 1583. His two sons were William and Theopolis :

EPITAPH OF JOHN CLAY, ESQUIRE.

"Soules they are made of Heavenly spirit :
From whence they come ye heavens inherite.
But know that body is made of Claye :
Death will devour by night and daye,
Yett is her as her was, I saye :
Ye livinge and dead remayneth Claye :
His very name that nature gave ;
Is now as shall be in his grave :
Tymes doth teache, experience tryes ;
That Claye to duste the winde updryes ;
Then this a wonder counpt we must ;
That want of winde should make Claye dust."

The Clay Arms are : Arg, a chev. engrailed between three trefoils slipt sable. Crest : Two wings expanded, arg, semes of trefoils slipped, sa.

These arms and crest are engraved on a silver tankard, brought over to this country by Robert Clay, Esquire, of Philadelphia, now in possession of the Booths of New Castle, Delaware.

NOTES.

The history of the Clay Family here given is mainly in accordance with its numerous traditions, corroborated by the court records of Chesterfield, Henrico, Hanover, Cumberland, Amelia, Powhatan, and Mecklenburg counties, Virginia, and Fayette, Bourbon, and Madison counties, Kentucky. We have found no illustrious ancestry, but a long line of worthy forbears, who, in most cases, bequeathed large estates to numerous children. We were not able to verify the tradition that the Emigrant was "Sir" John Clay, yet on October 1, 1765, in Chesterfield, and as late as 1780, in a suit before the High Court of Chancery (Judges Pendleton, Wythe, and Blair presiding), his great-great-grandson, Reverend John Clay, the father of Henry Clay, the Statesman, bore that title. Then, surely, Henry Clay, the "Mill-boy of the Slashes," was a mith, for the real Henry Clay was the son of an English nobleman and the heir to a good estate. This must be true, for the records give good history. Henry Clay was a clerk in the Chancery Court. Is this the reason he knew so little of family history? Who can solve the problem? I can offer but one suggestion. I believe Reverend John Clay received that title as a clergyman who had taken the degree of a Batchelor of Arts. All clergymen and priests were so designated in England at that time, and the custom prevailed in the Colonies to some extent. From the premises before me, this is my conclusion. Am I right or wrong?

Marston Clay, born 1746, married Elizabeth Williams, and through their son, James Williams Clay, and his wife, Clara Margaret Berry, were the ancestors of ex-Congressman James F. Clay, of Henderson, Kentucky. I believe this Marston identical with No. 14, and this his second marriage. He is evidently the grandson of Henry and Lucy Green Clay, of Cumberland County, Virginia.

ADDENDA.

GREEN FAMILY.

Thomas and Martha Green, the emigrants of this family, came to Virginia at an early period of her history, bringing with them two daughters (one of whom married —— Blocksom, and the other —— Eaton) and a son born upon the ocean en route to America, called "Thomas, the Seagull."

1. Thomas Green, "the Seagull," married Martha Filmer. daughter of Major Henry Filmer, a British officer, whose wife's name was Elizabeth, both of whom were born in England. Henry Filmer was a member of the House of Burgesses from Charles City County, 1642. (Hening's Statutes, Volume I.) Thomas and Martha (Filmer) Green had issue :

      I. JOHN GREEN ; married Elizabeth ——, and had Thomas Green (moved to South Carolina and left issue) and Elizabeth Green, who married a Payne and left issue.

2.   II. THOMAS GREEN.

    III. ELIZABETH GREEN; married John Crawley. Issue: Nathaniel Crawley ; Martha Crawley (married Thomas Cole, of Chickahominy River) ; Elizabeth Crawley (married —— Binns) ; Hannah Crawley ; Mary Crawley (married Samuel Terry, of Amelia County, Virginia).

    IV. REBECCA GREEN ; married (1) —— Condon ; (2) —— Marston. Had issue : Mary Condon (married William Booker, of Amelia), William Marston, Elizabeth Marston, Thomas Marston, and John Marston.

    V. MARY GREEN ; married (1) James Wilkerson ; (2) Thomas Walker. Issue : Priscilla and Sarah Wilkerson, Thomas and Elizabeth Walker.

    VI. COLONEL ABRAM GREEN, of Amelia County. Issue : Sally Green (married Terry Keen) ; Abram Green (married and left issue) ; Susanna Green (married —— Vodin) ; William Green (married —— Archer and left issue) ; and Obedience Green (married William Green).

VII. FILMER GREEN; married Mary Walker and had Elizabeth, Ann, Mary, Filmer, Edmund, and Susannah Green.

VIII. WILLIAM GREEN; married Amey Clay. Issue: Thomas, Patty (married William Williamson), Filmer, William, John, and Amey (married Edward Mosely, of Roanoke).

IX. HANNAH GREEN; married James Turner. Issue: Two sons, who died young.

---

2. Thomas Green, died 1730, married Elizabeth Marston, born November 25, 1672, died August 11, 1759, daughter and eldest child of Thomas and Elizabeth (Marvell) Marston. She survived her husband twenty-nine years. Signed her will November 12, 1758. It was probated January 24, 1760. They had issue:

I. A DAUGHTER; married Thomas Coles, or Cowles. Issue: Thomas Cowles.

II. ELIZABETH GREEN; married (1) —— Dawson, issue Samuel Dawson; (2) Leonard Cheatem, issue Leonard, Abey, Edward, and James Cheatem, and several daughters.

III. WILLIAM GREEN; died without issue.

IV. LUCY GREEN, born 1717; married Henry Clay in 1735.

V. MARTHA (PATSY) GREEN, born 1719; married Charles Clay in 1741.

3.   VI. THOMAS MARSTON GREEN; married Martha Wills and moved to Natchez, Mississippi, about 1776.

VII. REBECCA GREEN; married Frances Jones and moved to South Carolina.

VIII. MARSTON GREEN, of Amelia County, father of Grief Green, a prominent attorney.

---

3. Colonel Thomas Marston Green, of the Continental Army, was born in James City County, November 19, 1723, and married Martha Wills, November 21, 1752. She was born in 1734, and was the eldest daughter of Filmer Wills and his wife, Ann Harwood, daughter of William Harwood, a member of the Virginia Convention of 1776 from Warwick City County. Issue:

I. ELIZABETH GREEN, born October 21, 1753. No issue.

II. HENRY FILMER GREEN, born November 11, 1755. No issue.

4.   III. THOMAS MARSTON GREEN, JUNIOR, born February 6, 1758.

IV. ANTHONY GREEN, born January 1, 1760. No issue.

5.   V. ABNER GREEN, born January 21, 1762.

6.   VI. MARTHA WILLS GREEN, born December 25, 1763.
        VII. ANN HARWOOD GREEN, born December 17, 1765.
           (These seven born in Virginia.)
7.   VIII. HENRY M. GREEN, born November 8, 1767.
        IX. ELIAS GREEN, born October 9, 1769. No issue.
        X. FILMER W. GREEN, born April 6, 1772. No issue.
8.   XI. ABRAHAM GREEN, born September 28, 1774.
9.   XII. EVERARD GREEN, born April 15, 1776.

---

4. Thomas Marston Green, junior, born February 6, 1758; married Martha Kirkland. He represented the Mississippi Territory in the Seventh Congress of the United States, 1802-3. Issue:

    I. ELIZABETH GREEN; married John Davidson. Issue: Green, John, Filmer, and Martha Davidson.
    II. MARTHA GREEN; married John Hopkins. Issue:
        I. MARY HOPKINS; married Armstead Bradford.
        II. THOMAS HOPKINS; married Susanna Bisland. Issue: Thomas and Alexander Bisland.
    III. JOSEPH KIRKLAND GREEN, of Jefferson County, Mississippi; married, about 1803, Mildred Meriwether Cabell. Issue:
        I. MARTHA AUGUSTA GREEN, born January 31, 1806; married, January 8, 1829, Joseph Eggleston Jones. Issue: Twelve children — Joseph Cabell, Thomas Henry, Eugene D., Samuel Cabell, Sarah V., Archelaus Kirkland, William Syme, Meriwether Lewis, James Railey, Lucy A., and Meredith Dabney Jones. (See "The Cabells and their kin.")
        II. SAMUEL CABELL GREEN; married, in 1832, his cousin, Augusta Kirkland, daughter of Archibald Kirkland and his wife, Jane Green (sister of Joseph K. Green). No issue.
        III. LUCY ANN GREEN.
        IV. SARAH VIRGINIA GREEN; married Ammon Hancock, of Lynchburg, Virginia.
        V. THOMAS GREEN; died young.
    IV. MARY GREEN; married Charles Howell. Issue: Keziah Howell, married —— Foreman, and had Mary, Rebecca, Martha (married Rensen Holmes), and Richard Foreman.
    V. JANE GREEN; married Archibald Kirkland, and had Augusta, married (1) S. C. Green; (2) Blanton Ellis.
    VI. LAMINDA GREEN; married Major Thomas Hinds, of War of 1812, ancestor of Captain Thomas Hinds, Confederate States Army.

VII. REBECCA; married —— McCay.
VIII. WILLIAM GREEN; married Laura McCaleb.
IX. FILMER GREEN; married Emily McCaleb. Issue:
    I. WILLIAM GREEN. No issue.
    II. LAMINDA GREEN; married Robert Cox. Issue:
      William, Drusilla, Emily, Laura, Ernestine, Holmes, and Eva McCoy Cox.
X. AUGUSTA GREEN; married Rensen Holmes.

---

5. Abner Green, born January 21, 1762; died February 21, 1816. He married, November 1, 1784, Mary Hutchins (born February 4, 1768; died February 4, 1825), daughter of Colonel Anthony Pintard Hutchins (a British officer who was retired before the Revolutionary War), and his wife, Ann White. Issue:

I. THOMAS H. GREEN, born January 23, 1787. No issue.
II. JAMES GREEN, born February 24, 1789; married Mary Metcalfe.
III. MARY A. M. GREEN, born January 24, 1791; married Coles Meade April 7, 1807. Issue:
  I. COLES MEADE; married Sallie Wolfolk, daughter of Joseph Harris and Martha (Mitchell) Wolfolk, of Woodford County, Kentucky. Issue: Emma and Ada Meade. Ada married Daniel Saffrans, of Mississippi. Issue: Meade, Malvina, and Ada Saffrans.
  II. MARTHA MEADE, born October 14, 1826; married Samuel Fisher, 1840. Issue: Mary, who married Thomas White.
IV. ELIZA CELESTE GREEN, born November 26, 1792; married (1), Joseph Bowmar; (2), David Wood. Her daughter, Mary Caroline Bowmar, born June 5, 1814, married Doctor Charles Abercrombie, son of Reverend James Abercrombie, of Philadelphia, Pennsylvania. Issue five children, three of whom survive:
  I. ELIZA C. ABERCROMBIE; married J. J. Whoon, July 9, 1867. Issue.
  II. JOHN ABERCROMBIE, of Florida; has a very large family.
  III. MARY JOSEPHINE ABERCROMBIE, born April 14, 1841; married, August 2, 1865, Clifford Stanley Sims, born February 17, 1839, son of John Clarke and Emeline M. (Clarke) Sims. They reside at Mt. Holly, New Jersey. Issue: Charles A. Clifford, Launcelot, Ralph A., John Clarke, Thomson N., James Ross, and Ross Brainerd Sims.

V. CAROLINE C. GREEN ; married, May 17, 1814, Colonel Joseph Carson, who commanded a regiment of Mississippi Volunteers in the Creek War. He was born October 7, 1785, died May 27, 1817. Their son, James Green Carson, born March 8, 1815, died August 11, 1863 ; married, July 28, 1835, Catherine Waller, born January 20, 1815, died November 2, 1888, daughter of William S. Waller, of Frankfort, later of Lexington, Kentucky, in which two places he was for forty years the Cashier of the Bank of Kentucky. Issue :

 I. JOSEPH CARSON, born October 19, 1843.

 II. WILLIAM WALLER CARSON, born June 2, 1845 ; was a Confederate soldier, and at present is Professor of Civil Engineering in University of Tennessee.

 III. JAMES GREEN CARSON, born March 25, 1847, died unmarried, May 10, 1887.

 IV. EDWARD LEES CARSON, born August 12, 1848.

 V. KATHERINE BRECKINRIDGE CARSON, born February 20, 1853 ; married, November 21, 1876, Clifton R. Breckinridge, of Arkansas, late United States Minister to Russia. Issue : James Carson, Mary Carson, Susanna Preston, and Clifton Rhodes Breckinridge.

VI. MATILDA SUSAN GREEN ; married James Railey, of Versailles, Kentucky, son of Charles Railey and Mary Mayo, daughter of Colonel William Mayo, of Powhatan, Virginia, and had Mary Eliza Railey, born January 5, 1824, and married, January 24, 1844, Reverend Frederick W. Boyd, late Rector of the Episcopal Church at Waukesha, Wisconsin. Surviving issue :

 I. JAMES RAILEY BOYD, born August 13, 1846.

 II. WALTER STUART BOYD, born November 9, 1859.

 III. LOYD T. BOYD, born December 19, 1861 ; married Susan Patterson. Issue : Katherine Patterson Boyd.

 IV. CHARLES MAYO BOYD, born December 15, 1866.

6. Martha Wills Green ; married Cato West. Issue :

 I. MARTHA WEST ; married John Davidson.

 II. WILLIAM WEST ; married Sarah Kirkland.

 III. MARY WEST ; married Edward Turner.

 IV. THOMAS WEST, died unmarried.

 V. ELIZA WEST ; married —— McCoy.

 VI. JOHN WEST ; died unmarried.

 VII. ANNA WEST ; married Joseph Winn, of Franklin County, Mississippi.

VIII. SUSAN WEST ; married her cousin, Thomas West.
IX. CHARLES WEST ; married Charlotte Neilly, of Fayette, Mississippi.
X. CLAIBORNE WEST ; died unmarried.
XI. BENJAMIN West ; married Pauline Wing.

---

7. Henry M. Green ; married Jane Davidson, of Nashville, Tennessee. Their son, Thomas M. Green, of Vicksburg, married Mary Templeton. Issue :

I. MARY J. GREEN ; married Doctor William T. Stewart.
II. LUCY GREEN ; married William McCutcheon, of Vicksburg.
III. MARTHA GREEN ; married (1) —— Caviness ; (2) John Calderwood.
IV. JOHN GREEN (Confederate States Army) ; married Lizzie Harris.
V. MALVINA GREEN ; married Captain John W. Cobb.
VI. ROSANNA GREEN ; died unmarried.
VII. JOSEPH GREEN (Confederate States Army) ; died unmarried.
VIII. WILLIAM GREEN ; married Mary Paxton, of Vicksburg.

---

8. Abraham Green ; married Eliza Caffrey. Issue :

I. FILMER GREEN, born January 10, 1802.
II. THOMAS J. GREEN, born June 6, 1804.
III. MARY CAFFREY GREEN, born March 17, 1806.
IV. RACHEL JACKSON GREEN, born May 28, 1808.
V. JOHN DONALDSON GREEN, born June 8, 1810.
VI. ANDREW JACKSON GREEN, born January 31, 1812.
VII. ROBERT HAYS GREEN, born February 21, 1814.
VIII. MARTHA GREEN, born September 2, 1817.
IX. ABRAM ASBURY GREEN, born April 3, 1819.
X. ELIZA GREEN, born August 1, 1821.

---

9. Everard Green ; married Elizabeth Kirkland. Issue :

I. ELIZA KIRKLAND GREEN ; married Thomas Baker.
II. MARTHA W. GREEN ; married Doctor Eaton Kittredge.
III. LOUISA GREEN ; married Anthony Perryman.
IV. JOSEPH KIRKLAND GREEN ; married Fanny Ivy.
V. ELIZA J. GREEN ; married T. C. Ewing, of Kentucky.
VI. OCTAVIA C. GREEN ; married G. W. Race.
VII. ABNER GREEN ; married Sarah Wood, of Jefferson County. Mississippi, and lives at the home of the old Spanish General, Gayoso. They had, among other children, Payne Green, of Fort Gibson, Mississippi.

This Green history is culled from General Green Clay's manuscript, and later data contributed by Mrs. W. F. Boyd, of Waukesha, Wisconsin.

. THE WILL OF ELIZABETH (MARSTON) GREEN.

In the name of God, Amen. I, Elizabeth Green, of Nottoway Parish, Amelia County, being very sick and weak in body, but of sound and disposing mind and memory, yet considering the uncertainty of this mortal life, think it necessary to make and ordain this my last will and testament, which is as followeth :

I give and bequeath to my well-beloved son, Marston Green, the land and plantation whereon I now live, containing one hundred and fifty acres, be the same more or less, lying and being in Amelia County and joining the lines of Charles Irby, Richard Jones, William Fitzgerald, and William Hudson ; also two negroes, Cyrus and Bridget, to him and his heirs forever.

Item. I give and bequeath to my well-beloved daughter, Rebekah Jones, the feather bed and furniture whereon I now lye, and all my wearing apparel, both lining and wooling, and one dozen of the newest deep Pewter Plates, to her and her heirs forever.

Item. I give and bequeath to my grandson, Thomas Cowles, son of Thomas Coles, twenty shillings to buy him a gold mourning ring, to him and his heirs forever.

Item. I give to my granddaughter, Elizabeth Green, daughter of Thomas Green, twenty shillings, to buy her a gold mourning ring, to her and her heirs forever.

Item. I give and bequeath to my loving daughter, Lucy Clay, twenty shillings, to buy her a gold mourning ring.

Item. I give and bequeath to my loving daughter, Martha Clay, twenty shillings, to buy her a gold ring.

Item. I give and bequeath to my loving daughter, Elizabeth Cheatem, twenty shillings, to buy her a gold ring.

Item. I give and bequeath to my loving son, Marston Green, after my debts and the above legacies are paid, all the remainder part of my estate, both real and personal, to him and his heirs forever, and whom I likewise appoint my sole executor of this my last will and testament.

In witness whereof I have hereunto set my hand and seal this twelfth day of November, in the year of our Lord one thousand seven hundred and fifty-eight.   ELIZᴬ GREEN.

Signed, sealed, and acknowledged before us : Charles Irby, Abram Green, John Irby, Israel Marks.

At a court held for Amelia County, the 24th day of January, 1760, this will was proved by the oaths of Charles Irby, Abram Green, and John Irby, witnesses thereto, and sworn to by Marston Green, the executor herein named, and certificate was granted him for obtaining a probate in due form.

Test.   T. GRIFFIN PEACHY, County Clerk.

VAN HOOK FAMILY.

In the Dutch manuscripts at Albany, New York, Volume III, page 133, we find mention of Arent Isaacksen Van Hoeck in a document adjusting the terms of a lease between him and Pieter Jansen, July 9, 1655. He was one of the signers of the petition to Stuyvesant to surrender New Netherlands to the English on September 5, 1664.

On October 21, 1664, he was one of those who took the oath of allegiance to the English Government. He and his first wife, Geertje Everts, were members of the Reformed Dutch Church in 1649. (Collections of New York Historical, Genealogical, and Biographical Society, Volume I, page 29.) He married, August 9, 1665, Steyntje Laurens, widow of Jan. Hendricks.

Of this marriage, among other children, was Laurens Van Hoeck (Lawrence Van Hook), who was the first Dutchman to hold a judicial position in Monmouth County, New Jersey. (See "Old Times in Old Monmouth," by Salter & Beekman, page 269.)

He was Judge of Court of Quarter Sessions from November, 1715, to February, 1720.

Laurens Van Hoeck, "young man from New York," and Johannah Smit, "young daughter from Boschwych," married July 2, 1692, "both living here."

Johanna Smit was the daughter of Hendryck Barentze Smit and Geertje Willems (married June 2, 1663). Hendryck Barentze Smit emigrated from Lochem, Holland. He is represented in the Dutch Manuscripts, Volume III, page 131, as formerly a soldier in the service of the West India Company, in New Netherlands, and confers power of attorney on his brother, Dirk Smit, "at present ensign in the service of said company here" (and a very distinguished man in the colony).

Hendryck Barentze Smit is mentioned as a patentee in Governor Dongan's patent to Newtown. (Annals of Newtown, page 108, etc.)

He was appointed, August 18, 1673, a magistrate under the Dutch Government for Boswych (Bushwick), Long Island. (See O'Callahan's Register of New Netherlands, page 82.)

Judge Lawrence Van Hook and his wife, Johanna Smit, had, among other children, Frances, who married, in 1735, Reverend Samuel Blair, born June 14, 1712, died July 5, 1751, of Faggs Manor, Pennsylvania. He was descended from the Blairs of Ayrshire, Scotland.

Samuel Blair was educated under the Reverend William Tennant, and was licensed to preach November 9, 1733, by the Presbytery of Philadelphia.

He was installed pastor of New Londonderry, since known as Faggs Manor, April, 1740. Soon afterward he established there a classical and theological school, out of which grew the College of New Jersey.

He was a charter trustee of the College of New Jersey (now Princeton University). His zeal for the college made him travel when ill, and after a severe acute attack his health gradually failed. He died July 5, 1751. Reverend Samuel Davies spoke of him as "the incomparable Blair," and stated that in his travels in Great Britain he had heard no one equal to his instructor — not one whom he thought in any way to resemble or approach him in the matter or delivery of his sermons. Reverend Samuel Blair and his wife had eleven children :

I. JOSEPH BLAIR; died May 22, 1748, aged scarcely twelve years.

II. ELIZABETH BLAIR; married her cousin, the Reverend George Duffield, March 8, 1756.

III. MARY BLAIR, born 1739; married Reverend David Rice, of Virginia, June, 1763, and died in 1804, in Green County, Kentucky.

IV. REVEREND SAMUEL BLAIR, JUNIOR, born at Faggs Manor, Chester County, Pennsylvania, 1741; married, September 24, 1767, Susan, daughter of Doctor William Shippen, member of the Continental Congress from Germantown, Pennsylvania. In 1767 Mr. Blair was elected President of the College of New Jersey, and in 1790-2 was Chaplain of Congress.

V. WILLIAM LAWRENCE BLAIR, lawyer, early emigrant to Kentucky.

VI. HANNAH BLAIR, born 1745; died May 14, 1810; married Reverend William Foster, the great patriot of Octorara, Pennsylvania.

VII. SARAH BLAIR; married Rev. John Carmichael, of Pennsylvania.
VIII. FRANCES BLAIR; married James Moore, of Pennsylvania.
IX. MARTHA BLAIR; married Doctor Samuel Edmiston, of Pennsylvania.
X. SUSANNAH BLAIR; married Mr. Sanderson, of Pennsylvania.
XI. ISAAC BLAIR, died young, July 30, 1752.

THE MACCOUN FAMILY.

1. James Maccoun, the first known ancestor of the Kentucky family of this name, was born in Linlithgowshire, midway between Glasgow and Edinburgh, Scotland, in 1639. His ancestors were Danes, being adventurers into Scotland during the Danish invasions of the tenth century. He married Elizabeth Montgomery, of the "Montgomerys of Lainshaw"; was a soldier under William III, and fell at the Battle of the Boyne, in Ireland, July 1, 1690. Issue:

2. James Maccoun, junior, born 1660; married his cousin, Mary Campbell, of the "Campbells of Lochow." Issue:

3. James Maccoun (III), born 1717, in Antrim, Ireland, where his father had settled while a soldier under King William and Mary. He emigrated to Virginia in 1742. Landed at Norfolk, and settled on the Catawba in Botetourt County, Virginia. Here he married Margaret Walker, in April, 1744. She was a woman of great energy and fine judgment, and possessed a strong, beautiful voice, and, while not permitted to "pitch the tunes," she led the singing at the church at "the Peaks of Otter" in Virginia, of which Reverend David Rice was the pastor. Mr. Rice came to Kentucky in 1783. June 4, 1784, he preached the funeral sermon of Margaret (Walker) Maccoun, which was the first sermon ever preached on the banks of Salt River. James Maccoun, senior, was the first elder of the First Presbyterian Church (New Providence) founded by Mr. Rice in Kentucky. (See Davidson's Presbyterianism in Kentucky.) James Maccoun was a soldier of the Revolution and the senior member of the McAfee Company, which left Botetourt County, Virginia, May 10, 1773,

and reached Salt River, Mercer County, Kentucky, July 21, 1773. His will was probated at Harrodsburg, Kentucky, in October, 1800. Issue :

4.
 I. JAMES MACCOUN, born March 11, 1745.
 II. ANN MACCOUN, born August 1, 1746; married Robert McAfee. They were the parents of General Robert Breckinridge McAfee, the historian.
 III. SAMUEL MACCOUN, born October 20, 1748; died young.
 IV. MARY MACCOUN, born August 13, 1750; married John Magee.
 V. SUSAN MACCOUN, born April 7, 1752; married James Maccoun, of South Carolina.
 VI. JOHN MACCOUN, born March 28, 1754; married Elizabeth Tilford.
 VII. JANE MACCOUN, born May 1, 1756; married (1) John Wood; (2) Samuel Adams, junior.
 VIII. MARGARET MACCOUN, born April 15, 1758; married —— Kerr.
 IX. ELIZABETH MACCOUN, born February 7, 1761; married John Ledgerwood.
 X. JOSEPH MACCOUN was born February 19, 1763. While watching some cattle in a glade he was surprised and captured by a party of Shawnee Indians and carried to the headwaters of Mad River, about six miles above the spot now occupied by Springfield, Ohio, where he endured excruciating tortures and was burned at the stake in March, 1781.

4. James Maccoun, born March 11, 1745; married Anne Tilford (sister of Jeremiah Tilford, the ancestor of the Tilfords and Boyles, of Boyle and Fayette counties, Kentucky). He was a Revolutionary soldier in Captain Rowland's Company of Virginia troops, June 10, 1777, and a member of the McAfee Company, early pioneers of Kentucky. His will, probated at Harrodsburg, Kentucky, December, 1790, mentions as legatees, wife, Ann, sons, James, John, and David, and daughters, Elizabeth, Ann, Margaret, and Mary. Of these:

5. James Maccoun (fifth of the name in direct succession) was born in Botetourt County, Virginia, in 1767; died in Paris, Kentucky, 1832. Was an early settler at Lexington, and one of her most enterprising citizens, being one of the Trustees of

Transylvania University, 1783 ; one of the founders of the Public Library in 1805, and of the Kentucky Eastern Lunatic Asylum (Fayette Hospital) in 1816, the first three institutions of their kind in the State. He was an elder of the Presbyterian Church. He married, in Mercer County, Kentucky, October 21, 1797, Elizabeth Rice (born in Bedford County, Virginia, January 10, 1774, died in Paris, Kentucky, February 18, 1833), daughter of Reverend David Rice and his wife, Mary Blair, daughter of Reverend Samuel Blair, of Faggs Manor, Pennsylvania. Reverend David Rice, son of David and grandson of Thomas Rice, the emigrant, was born in Hanover County, Virginia, December 20, 1733 ; ordained by Hanover Presbytery, December, 1763 ; was a distinguished patriot of the Revolution, and a member of the Committee of Safety for Bedford County, May, 1775 ; was one of the founders of the Hampden-Sidney College ; emigrated to Kentucky in 1773, and became the father of Presbyterianism in the State. He was the moving spirit and one of the charter members of Transylvania Seminary, and Chairman of the Board of Trustees for many years. The school was opened in his house, in Lincoln County, and his son-in-law, Reverend James Mitchell, was its first teacher. David Rice was recently called the "wisest statesman of his day and the most learned man in Kentucky." He left numerous descendants in Virginia and Kentucky. He died June 18, 1816. The Presbyterian Church of Kentucky has erected a beautiful monument to him and his wife in the city park at Danville.

James and Elizabeth Maccoun had ten children, only two of whom left descendants :

> I. ARABELLA ANNE TILFORD MACCOUN, born October 2, 1802 ; died May 30, 1828 ; married, June, 1818, Colonel L. B. Clay. Issue : Henry, Olivia, Elizabeth, and Samuel Clay.
>
> II. PAUL MACCOUN, born October 11, 1816 ; died 1888 ; married, September 22, 1842, Catherine Potts, born July 8, 1826 ; died April 2, 1876. Issue : Martha, Mary, Lutie, and James Rice Bush Maccoun.

HART FAMILY.

1. Thomas Hart, the immigrant, came from England to Hanover County, Virginia, about the close of the seventeenth century. He married Susanna Rice, the daughter of Thomas Rice, an Englishman of Welch extraction, an early adventurer into Virginia, who settled in Hanover. Mr. Hart died in that county in 1755. They had issue :

2.   I. THOMAS HART; married Susanna Gray, of North Carolina. In 1794 he came to Lexington, Kentucky, where he died June 23, 1809, "an old and very respectable inhabitant of this place" (Kentucky Gazette). His will was probated in Fayette County, July, 1809. Mrs. Hart died in Lexington in 1832.

     II. JOHN HART; settled and died in Henderson, Kentucky. He married Miss Lane, of Hanover County, Virginia. Issue : Thomas.

     III. BENJAMIN HART; settled in Missouri.

     IV. DAVID HART, of North Carolina; married Miss Nunn.

     V. NATHANIEL HART, born in 1714; married Sarah Simpson in 1740. His home was "Red House," Caswell County, North Carolina. He settled at Boonesborough, Kentucky, in 1779, near which place he was killed by the Indians in 1785.

     VI. A DAUGHTER, name unknown; married James Gooch, of Georgia. Their daughter, Ann, married Colonel Jesse Benton, and died in St. Louis, Missouri, in 1837. A son, James Gooch, remained in Georgia. Colonel Jesse Benton and Ann Gooch were the parents of Honorable Thomas H. Benton, who for thirty years was United States Senator from Missouri.

2. Thomas Hart and Susanna Gray had issue :

     I. THOMAS HART; married Nellie Grosch, of Hagerstown, Maryland.

     II. NATHANIEL GRAY HART; married Ann Gist, daughter of Thomas Gist, of Bourbon County. He became Captain of the Lexington Light Infantry, which was organized May 11, 1812. They were called the "Silk Stocking Boys," and were attached to the Fifth Regiment of Kentucky Volunteer Militia, commanded by Colonel William Lewis. Captain Nathaniel G. T. Hart was captured by the Indians at the Battle of the River Raisin, January 22, 1813. Issue :

I. THOMAS HART; died unmarried.
II. HENRY HART; married Elizabeth Brent, daughter
        of Hugh and Elizabeth (Langhorne) Brent, of
        Paris, Kentucky, and settled in St. Louis, Mis-
        souri. Their children were:
    I. ELIZABETH HART; unmarried.
    II. NATHANIEL G. HART.
    III. HUGH HART; married Nannie Fry. Issue:
            Elizabeth Hart, married Walter Gage.
            Issue: Mary Bartley Gage.
    IV. HENRY HART.
III. JOHN HART, who died in St. Louis, Missouri, in 1820.
IV. ELIZA HART, born September 9, 1768, died in Hagerstown,
        Maryland, August, 1798; married Doctor Richard Pin-
        dell, a surgeon in the Maryland line of the Revolutionary
        army, who died in Lexington, Kentucky, March 16, 1833.
V. SUSANNA HART; married Samuel Price, and died in Louis-
        ville in 1865. Issue:
    I. NANETTE PRICE; married Thomas Smith, and
            died in Louisville in 1878.
    II. ELIZA PRICE; married Honorable Thomas A.
            Marshall, born in Woodford County, Kentucky,
            January 15, 1794, and died in Louisville, April
            16, 1871.
VI. NANCY HART; married Honorable James Brown (son of
        Honorable John and Margaret (Preston) Brown), born
        September 11, 1766, in Virginia.
VII. LUCRETIA HART, born March 18, 1781; married Honorable
        Henry Clay.

JACOB FAMILY.

John Jacob, senior, the ancestor of the Jacob family in this
country, emigrated from Hampshire, England, in the year 1665,
and settled in Anne Arundel County, Maryland. From the earliest times the name of Jacob was known in the south of England and the Isle of Wight, and mention is made of them as
being the King's Thanes.

In this country the Jacob family has always borne an honored
name, and many members have held positions of trust. Among
them the late John I. Jacob, of West Virginia, was Governor of
that State and judge of one of the higher courts. Richard T.

Jacob was a Colonel in the Federal Army during the Civil War, and was afterward Lieutenant Governor of Kentucky. The Honorable Charles D. Jacob was three times Mayor of Louisville and Minister to the United States of Colombia.

John I. Jacob, of Louisville, was born in Romney, Hampshire County, Virginia, in 1788, and died April 1, 1852. He married, as his second wife, Lucy Donald Robertson, the daughter of Isaac Robertson, a graduate of Princeton and a lawyer by profession, whose father was Donald Robertson, the son of Charles Robertson, of Inverness, Scotland. They belonged to the Robertson Clan, noted in the Wars of Montrose.

Donald, the first of the family in this country, was born at Inverness, September 27, 1717, and was graduated from the University of Edinburgh. His father lived at the Mar, in the enjoyment of an ample fortune, but after the terrible defeat of the Scots at Culloden, in 1746, he lost his estate, and a short time after removed to Sunderland, England, where he died in 1757. His son, Donald, came to America in 1752 and established a private school at Drysdale, King and Queen County, Virginia, which soon grew into an academy of note.

In 1764 he married Rachel Rogers, daughter of John Rogers and Mary Boyd, and sister of Ann Rogers, the mother of George Rogers Clarke, by whom he had three children — Charles, Lucy, and Isaac. Isaac was the father of Lucy Robertson, the mother of Susanna Jacob.

The mother of Lucy Robertson and grandmother of Susanna Jacob was Matilda Taylor, the daughter of Commodore Richard Taylor, the son of Colonel George Taylor, member of the Virginia House of Burgesses.

BRODHEAD FAMILY.

Daniel Brodhead, the immigrant from Yorkshire, came as an English soldier to New York, settled at Watertown, and died there July 14, 1667. He was commissioned Captain of Musketeers by Charles II, and served under Colonel Richard Nichols, who, in May, 1664, captured New Netherlands (New York) from the Dutch. Captain Brodhead commanded the English forces at Kingston, New York, September 14, 1665. He subsequently returned to England and brought his wife and two children to America. He married Ann, daughter of Francis and Letos (Solomon) Tye. After Captain Brodhead's death she married, in 1674, Captain William Nottingham, and bore him William, Elizabeth, and John. Captain Nottingham died June 1, 1680, and, in 1681, Ann married Thomas Garton, and had issue: Ann, who died unmarried. Captain and Ann Brodhead had issue: Charles and Daniel.

Charles Brodhead was born in England; came with his parents and brother to America and settled at Marbletown, Ulster County, New York, dying there March 12, 1724. He was commissioned Ensign in Captain Thomas Garton's Company August 30, 1685 (commission signed by Thomas Dongan). He married, November 14, 1693, Maria Ten Broeck, daughter of Wessell Ten Broeck, born 1635, and married, December 17, 1670, to Maria Ten Eyck, of Kingston, New York, who was in New Amsterdam in 1651. Wessell Ten Broeck came to America in 1659. Charles and Maria (Ten Broeck) Brodhead had issue — a son — Daniel Brodhead, who was born and resided at Marbletown; was baptized November 11, 1694, and died 1759–61. He was commissioned Lieutenant of Colonel Levi Paulding's Company June 2, 1726 (commission signed by Governor William Burnet); promoted Captain April 20, 1733 (commission signed by Governor William Cosby). He was married December 20, 1755, to Mariche Koch, who was baptized August 7, 1726, and died March 5, 1804. She was the daughter of Samuel and Bridger (Middag) Koch, who were married June 17, 1722. Captain Daniel and Mariche (Koch) Brodhead had issue:

I. SAMUEL BRODHEAD; married Dinah Dubois.
II. DANIEL BRODHEAD, who was born near Marbletown, and
baptized September 26, 1756, and died August 10, 1831.
He was commissioned Ensign of the Grenadier Com-
pany, Third New York Regiment, February 21, 1778;
Lieutenant, June 21, 1786 (commission signed by George
Clinton); Captain, April 10, 1798 (commission signed
by John Jay). He married, March 5, 1778, Blandina
Elmendorf, who died March 13, 1848, aged eighty-seven
years. She was the daughter of Johnathan and Hellena
(Smedes) Elmendorf. Johnathan Elmendorf was commissioned Lieutenant Colonel of the First or Northern
Regiment of New York troops, February 19, 1778, and
resigned November 2, 1781. Colonel Johnathan was
the son of Major Conrad Elmendorf and Blandina
Kiersted, daughter of Doctor Ruelof Kiersted, son of
Doctor Hans Kiersted and Sarah R. *Jansen*, daughter
of Anneke *Janse*. Captain Daniel and Blandina Brodhead had issue:

> LUCAS BRODHEAD, born at Marbletown, October 31,
> 1793; died October 31, 1849. He was grad-
> uated from Union College, Schenectady, New
> York, in class of 1816; studied law at Albany,
> and moved to Kentucky about 1820 and prac-
> ticed his profession until his death. He mar-
> ried, December 20, 1832, Mary Cordelia Upshaw
> Price, daughter of Richard Price (a soldier in
> the War of 1812, who died in service) and
> Hannah Upshaw, of Virginia, daughter of John
> and Mary (Lafon) Upshaw. Richard Price was
> the son of Samuel Price, of Maryland, and Eliza-
> beth Richardson, daughter of William Richardson
> and Isabella, daughter of Marquis Calmes, a
> Huguenot. John Upshaw was a member of the
> House of Burgesses, 1758–65; signer of the
> articles of the Westmoreland Association, 1766,
> and Chairman of the Committee of Safety, 1775.
> Lucas and Mary (Price) Brodhead were the
> parents of Lucas Brodhead, of Spring Station,
> Kentucky, who was born at Frankfort, Kentucky,
> April 12, 1844, and married, June 29, 1880, Sallie
> Watson Breck, daughter of Doctor Robert Levi
> Breck, who was born May 8, 1827, and married
> (1), June 21, 1847, Martha G. Rodes, daughter of
> Colonel William and Pauline Green (Clay) Rodes.
> Doctor Breck was son of Judge Daniel Breck,
> of the Court of Appeals, and member of Con-

gress from Kentucky (born February 12, 1788, and died February 4, 1871), and married, June 2, 1819, Jane Briggs Todd (born June 3, 1796, and died June 30, 1852), daughter of General Levi Todd (born October 4, 1756; died 1808), who married, September 25, 1779, Jane Briggs (died 1803), daughter of Samuel and Sarah Logan (sister of General Benjamin Logan), and daughter of David and Jane Logan. General Todd was son of David Todd (born April 8, 1723, died February 8, 1785), who married Hannah Owen, and grandson of Robert and —— Smith Todd. Judge Breck was son of Reverend Daniel Breck, a Chaplain in the Revolutionary War (born August 18, 1748; died August 12, 1845); married Hannah, daughter of Elijah and Dorothy Porter. Reverend Daniel Breck was son of John and Margaret (Thomas) Breck, and grandson of John and Ann (Pattershall) Breck.

Mr. Lucas Brodhead, of Spring Station, has in his possession the original commissions of most of these distinguished soldiers.

AUTHORITIES.

Virginia Magazine of History; Richmond Critic; Hotten's Immigrants; William and Mary Quarterly; Colonel William Russell and His Descendants; Governor Garrard and His Descendants; Cooke's Virginia; County Records of Chesterfield, Hanover, Henrico, Charles City, Lunenburg, Franklin, and Amelia; Old Tombstones; Family Bibles; Register of Land Offices of Virginia and Kentucky; The Cabells and Their Kin, etc.

INDEX TO PART FIRST.

INDEX TO THE GENEALOGY OF THE CLAYS.

THE

FILSON CLUB PUBLICATIONS.

The Filson Club is an historical, biographical, and literary association located in Louisville, Kentucky. It was named after John Filson, the first historian of Kentucky, whose quaint little octavo of one hundred and eighteen pages was published at Wilmington, Delaware, in 1784. It was organized May 15, 1884, and incorporated October 5, 1891, for the purpose, as expressed in its charter, of collecting, preserving, and publishing the history of Kentucky and adjacent States, and cultivating a taste for historic inquiry and study among its members. While its especial field of operations was thus theoretically limited, its practical workings were confined to no locality. Each member is at liberty to choose a subject and prepare a paper and read it to the Club, among whose archives it is to be filed. From the papers thus accumulated selections are made for publication, and there have now been issued fourteen volumes or numbers of these publications. They are all paper bound quartos, printed with pica old-style type, on pure white antique paper, with broad margins and halftone illustrations. They have been admired both at home and abroad, not only for their original and valuable matter, but also for their tasteful and comely appearance. They are not printed for sale in the commercial sense of the term, but for free distribution among the members of the Club. There are always, however, some numbers left over after the members are supplied, which are either exchanged with other societies or sold. The following is a brief descriptive list of all the Club publications to date :

The Filson Club Publications.

1. JOHN FILSON, the first historian of Kentucky: An account of his life and writings, principally from original sources. Prepared for The Filson Club and read at its second meeting in Louisville, Kentucky, June 26, 1884, by Reuben T. Durrett, A. M., LL.D., President of the Club. Illustrated with a likeness of Filson, a *fac-simile* of one of his letters, and a photo-lithographic reproduction of his map of Kentucky printed at Philadelphia in 1784. 4to, 132 pages. John P. Morton & Co., Printers, Louisville, Kentucky. 1884.

2. THE WILDERNESS ROAD, a description of the routes of travel by which the pioneers and early settlers first came to Kentucky. Prepared for The Filson Club by Captain Thomas Speed, Secretary of the Club. Illustrated with a map showing the roads of travel. 4to, 75 pages. John P. Morton & Co., Printers, Louisville, Kentucky. 1886.

3. THE PIONEER PRESS OF KENTUCKY, from the printing of the first paper west of the Alleghanies, August 11, 1787, to the establishment of the Daily Press, 1830. Prepared for The Filson Club by William Henry Perrin, member of the Club. Illustrated with *fac-similes* of the Kentucky Gazette and the Farmer's Library, a view of the first printing house in Kentucky, and likenesses of John Bradford, Shadrack Penn, and George D. Prentice. 4to, 93 pages. John P. Morton & Co., Printers, Louisville, Kentucky. 1888.

4. LIFE AND TIMES OF JUDGE CALEB WALLACE, some time a Justice of the Court of Appeals of the State of Kentucky. By William H. Whitsitt, D. D., member of The Filson Club. 4to, 151 pages. John P. Morton & Co., Printers, Louisville, Kentucky. 1888.

5. AN HISTORICAL SKETCH OF ST. PAUL'S CHURCH, Louisville, Kentucky, prepared for the Semi-Centennial Celebration, October 6, 1889. By Reuben T. Durrett, A. M., LL.D., President of The Filson Club. Illustrated with likenesses of Reverend William Jackson and Reverend Edmund T. Perkins, D. D., and views of the church as first built in 1839 and as it appeared in 1889. 4to, 90 pages. John P. Morton & Co., Printers, Louisville, Kentucky. 1889.

6. THE POLITICAL BEGINNINGS OF KENTUCKY: A narrative of public events bearing on the history of the State up to the time of its admission into the American Union. By Colonel John Mason Brown, member of The Filson Club. Illustrated with a likeness of the author. 4to, 263 pages. John P. Morton & Co., Printers, Louisville, Kentucky. 1889.

7. THE CENTENARY OF KENTUCKY. Proceedings at the celebration by The Filson Club, Wednesday, June 1, 1892, of the one hundredth anniversary of the admission of Kentucky as an independent State into the Federal Union. Prepared for publication by Reuben T. Durrett, A. M., LL.D., President of the Club. Illustrated with likenesses of President Durrett, Major Stanton, Sieur LaSalle, and General Clark, and *fac-similes* of the music and songs at the centennial banquet. 4to, 200 pages. John P. Morton & Co., Printers, Louisville, Kentucky. 1892.

8. THE CENTENARY OF LOUISVILLE. A paper read before the Southern Historical Association, Saturday, May 1, 1880, in commemoration of the one hundredth anniversary of the beginning of the City of Louisville as an incorporated town under an act of the Virginia Legislature. By Reuben T. Durrett, A. M., LL.D., President of The Filson Club. Illustrated with likenesses of Colonel Durrett, Sieur LaSalle, and General Clark. 4to, 200 pages. John P. Morton & Co., Printers, Louisville, Kentucky. 1893.

9. THE POLITICAL CLUB, Danville, Kentucky, 1786–1790: Being an account of an early Kentucky debating society from the original papers recently found. By Captain Thomas Speed, Secretary of The Filson Club. 4to, xii–167 pages. John P. Morton & Co., Printers, Louisville, Kentucky. 1894.

10. THE LIFE AND WRITINGS OF RAFINESQUE. Prepared for The Filson Club and read at its meeting, Monday, April 2, 1894. By Richard Ellsworth Call, M. A., M. Sc., M. D., member of The Filson Club. Illustrated with likenesses of Rafinesque and *fac-similes* of pages of his Fishes of the Ohio and Botany of Louisville. 4to, xii–227 pages. John P. Morton & Co., Printers, Louisville, Kentucky. 1895.

11. TRANSYLVANIA UNIVERSITY: Its origin, rise, decline, and fall. Prepared for The Filson Club by Robert Peter, M. D.,

and his daughter, Miss Johanna Peter, members of The Filson
Club. Illustrated with a likeness of Doctor Peter. 4to, 202 pages.
John P. Morton & Co., Printers, Louisville, Kentucky. 1896.

12. BRYANT'S STATION and the memorial proceedings held on
its site under the auspices of the Lexington Chapter, D. A. R.,
August 18, 1896, in honor of its heroic mothers and daughters.
Prepared for publication by Reuben T. Durrett, A. M., LL.D.,
President of The Filson Club. Illustrated with likenesses of the
officers of the Lexington Chapter, D. A. R., President Durrett,
Major Stanton, Professor Rancke, Colonel Young, and Doctor
Todd, and full-page views of Bryant's Station and its spring, and
of the battlefield of the Blue Licks. 4to, xiii – 277 pages. John
P. Morton & Co., Printers, Louisville, Kentucky. 1897.

13. THE FIRST EXPLORATIONS OF KENTUCKY: The journal
of Doctor Thomas Walker, 1750, and of Colonel Christopher
Gist, 1751. Edited by Colonel J. Stoddard Johnston, Vice-Pres-
ident of The Filson Club. Illustrated with a map of Kentucky
showing the routes of Walker and Gist through the State, with
a view of Castle Hill, the residence of Doctor Walker, and a
likeness of Colonel Johnston. 4to, 256 pages. John P. Morton
& Co., Printers, Louisville, Kentucky. 1898.

14. THE CLAY FAMILY. Part First — The Mother of Henry
Clay, by Zachary F. Smith, member of The Filson Club; Part
Second — The Genealogy of the Clays, by Mrs. Mary Rogers
Clay, member of The Filson Club. Illustrated with a full-page
halftone likeness of Henry Clay, of each of the authors, and a
full-page picture of the Clay coat-of-arms; also four full-page
grouped illustrations, each containing four likenesses of members
of the Clay family. 4to, vi – 276 pages. John P. Morton & Co.,
Printers, Louisville, Kentucky. 1899.

Printed in the USA
CPSIA information can be obtained
at www.ICGtesting.com
LVHW081241161023
761215LV00017B/1577